WARBIRDS
OF WORLD WAR II

WARBIRDS
OF WORLD WAR II

JEFFREY L. ETHELL

CRESTLINE

This edition published in 2013 by
CRESTLINE
a division of BOOK SALES, INC.
276 Fifth Avenue Suite 206
New York, New York 10001
USA

This edition published in 2003 by Crestline, an imprint of MBI Publishing Company LLC, 400 First Avenue North, Suite 400, Minneapolis, Minnesota, 55401

First published by MBI Publishing Company.

ISBN-13: 978-0-7858-2970-6

Front cover: This flight of advanced transition fighters out of Randolph Field, Texas, consists of a P-40K, a P-40R-1, and a P-40R-2. *USAF*

Front banner (left to right): These pilots of B Flight, 87th Squadron, 79th Fighter Group at Rentschler Field, Connecticut, were transferred intact from the 65th Squadron, 57th Fighter Group when the 57th was moved overseas in early July 1942. *Charles Jaslow*

The need for night fighters led to a contract for Lockheed to modify 75 P-38L-5s to P-38M-6 Night Lightnings with AN/APS-4 radar and a second seat for an observer. *USAF*

John P. "Jeep" Crowder flying a 524th Squadron A-36A in 1943 over Mt. Etna, Sicily.

A 36th Squadron, 8th Pursuit Group pilot climbs into the squadron commander's P-40 at Langley. *USAF*

On the frontispiece: A 1st Fighter Group pilot climbs aboard his P-38D during the Carolina Manuevers in late 1941.

On the title page: A 339th Fighter Group P-51D, *Arrow Head*, visits Mt. Farm, England, in late 1944 from its base at Fowlmere. *Robert Astrella*

Back cover: Pilot and radar observer climb into a P-38M Night Lightning. The observer had to be small of stature in order to fit into the tiny rear cockpit. *USAF*

Contents

P-38 LIGHTNING

P-40 WARHAWK

P-52 MUSTANG

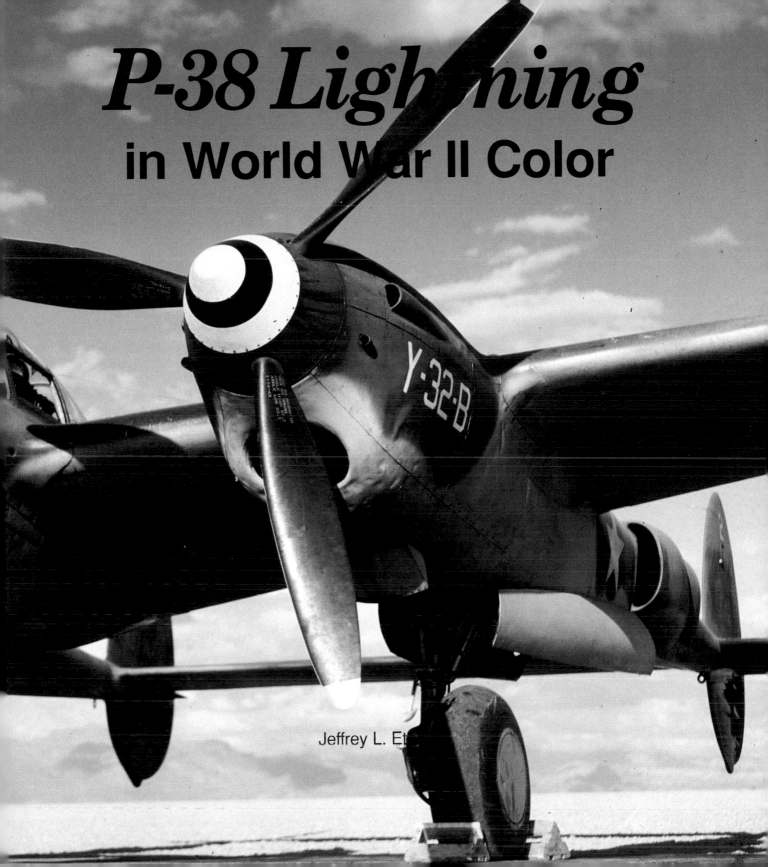

P-38 Lightning
in World War II Color

Jeffrey L. Eth

Introduction

Gathering Storm

In the isolationist climate of the 1930s, military aviation budgets suffered severely. Industries improved on older aircraft models rather than build entirely new machines. Yet some visionaries in the services saw the coming world war and realized the United States was ill-prepared. In February 1937, the US Army Air Corps requested proposals for a new type of aircraft, an "interceptor." Congress deemed the idea acceptable because it sounded like a purely defensive weapon, one that would intercept incoming enemy bombers at high altitude.

The Air Corps asked for a major breakthrough in performance: They wanted a minimum true air speed of 360mph at high altitude and the ability to reach 20,000ft in six minutes. Unfortunately, there were no American aircraft engines available with the horsepower to give an airplane such performance figures. The only engine that came close was the Allison V-1710-C8, which had yet to be tested at 1,000hp. At the time,

there wasn't sufficient money for further engine development.

Using the Allison engine, there were two approaches to the problem: build a larger fighter around two of the engines or make an airframe as light as possible using one engine. Fortunately, American manufacturers had an ally in Lt. Benjamin S. Kelsey, the chief of Wright Field's Pursuit Projects Office. Kelsey had coined the term interceptor so the Army could get the fighter it needed without Congress knowing enough to interfere.

Only two proposals were submitted in response to the Army's request—Lockheed's Model 22 (later to become the XP-38) and Bell's Model 4 (later to become the XP-39). Lockheed's Clarence L. "Kelly" Johnson took the more radical approach of designing a twin-boomed, twin-engine fighter that was 150 percent larger than normal. Bell's Bob Woods, on the other hand, put a single engine behind the cockpit, on webs that served as engine mount, wing spar, and landing gear trunion to get a 20 percent reduction in weight. Prototypes were ordered in June and October 1937, respectively.

In July 1938 construction of the XP-38 was initiated using two Allison C-9 engines (later V-1710-11 and -15) rated at 1,090hp each. The right engine turned its propeller "backward" (clockwise when viewed from the front) so the two propellers counter rotated, each engine canceling the effect of the other engine's torque. Maximum weight was projected at over 15,000lb. The new fighter was striking, a vast leap ahead in technology: tricycle landing gear, high wing loading, Fowler flaps for low-speed handling, butt jointed and flush riveted skin, bubble canopy, and metal covered control surfaces.

After the XP-38 was completed in December 1938, it was disassembled, covered, and trucked to March Field, California, during the early morning of January 1, 1939. Kelsey began taxi tests on January 9 and made the first flight on January 27 after delays caused by brake problems and flap flutter. Overall, Kelsey was delighted with the airplane, particularly since it was well within performance requirements. On February 11, after about five hours' total flying time, Kelsey made a speed run to Wright Field, averaging 360mph at cruise power.

Chief of the Army Air Corps, Gen. Henry H. "Hap" Arnold, was there to meet him. He told Kelsey to refuel, fly to Mitchel Field, Long Island, and establish a transcontinental speed record, something he hoped

would sell the fighter to Congress. The next leg went flawlessly but, due to the flap flutter and weak-brake problems that had not been ironed out of the prototype, Kelsey had to drag the aircraft in on final approach at minimum speed. Apparently, carburetor ice had formed, leaving the power at idle regardless of throttle movement. Kelsey hit the ground short of the field resulting in the total loss of the XP-38, though he came away unscathed. Arnold took Kelsey to Washington the next day and, fortunately, they sold the program based on Kelsey's reports. Sixty days later, Lockheed had a contract for thirteen service test YP-38s.

Lightning Strike

The first YP flew on September 16, 1940 (the Army had already ordered 673 based on performance estimates) with the last YP being delivered eight months later. By the end of 1941, another 196 aircraft had been delivered, though none were combat capable. Flight testing revealed a problem that was to dog the aircraft through most of its career: compressibility in a dive. Not until dive flaps were added to the J and L models, beginning in June 1944, were pilots allowed to enter prolonged dives. Tail flutter, caused by the sharp junction of wings and fuselage pod, was solved by the installation of large fairings that smoothed the airflow. Though elevator mass balances had been fitted as one of the fixes to this problem, Kelly Johnson insisted they never made any difference.

By the end of October 1941, the first combat equipped version, the P-38E, rolled off the production lines, succeeded by the P-38F in April 1942. The first production aircraft were named Atlanta by Lockheed. Fortunately, the British, who had ordered the type, thought Lightning was a better name and it stuck by October 1941. Unfortunately, the British Model 322 Lightnings were devoid of turbosuperchargers and counter rotating propellers, robbing the fighter of its finest performance features. The Air Ministry canceled its order for 667 Lightnings, but the 143 that had been produced were turned over to the US Army Air Forces for training after being refitted with counter rotating propellers.

Flying the new fighter was a challenge for inexperienced pilots. At full power on takeoff, if one engine failed, full opposite rudder could not keep it from rolling over into the ground. The developed procedure was to reduce power on the good engine, regain control, feather the prop on the dead engine, trim the yaw out, then come back up on the power. Pilots who were not quick enough were killed, resulting in an initial bad reputation for the P-38.

Lightning Storm

With the P-38E, armament was standardized at one 20mm cannon and four .50 caliber machine guns. An additional ninety-nine Es were built as F-4 photographic-reconnaissance aircraft with cameras in place of guns in the nose. These were the first Lightnings to enter combat. In April 1942, they were flown out of Australia, then Port Moresby, New Guinea, with the 8th Photo Reconnaissance Squadron under Maj. Karl Polifka. By June, P-38Es were flying combat missions with the 54th Fighter Squadron up and down the 1,200 mile Aleutian chain in some of the worst weather in the world. From the P-38F production line came F-4As and F-5As; the new F-5 designation remained for all subsequent recce birds.

By November 1942, the P-38F was in action over North Africa with the Twelfth Air Force after being flown across the North Atlantic by the 1st and 14th Fighter Groups, initially attached to the Eighth Air Force. North Africa was a bitter, forsaken theater of operations, hard on both pilots and planes. Seasoned German fighter pilots whittled the Lightnings down as American pilots tried to gain experience as well as prove their new fighters. One of these pilots was the author's father, Lt. E. C. Ethell, 48th Fighter Squadron, 14th Fighter Group. By December, the 3rd Photo Reconnaissance Group, flying F-4s and F-5As, as well as the 82nd Fighter Group, had arrived in North Africa with Lightnings.

In November 1942, the 39th Fighter Squadron took the Lightning into combat over New Guinea, and the 339th Fighter Squadron started flying over the Solomon Islands from the airstrips on Guadalcanal. Evident right away was the inability of the P-38 to outmaneuver the Zero. For the first time, however, superior climb rate, concentrated fire power, and long range put American fighter pilots on the offensive, able to choose when to engage in combat or when to refuse. By December 1942, the 70th Fighter Squadron and the 17th Photo Squadron had arrived at Guadalcanal while the 9th Fighter Squadron was equipped with Lightnings at Port Moresby in January 1943. In March, the 80th Fighter Squadron began operations with the Fifth Air Force out of New Guinea.

On April 18, 1943, a formation of 70th and 339th Squadron P-38s out of Guadalcanal, led by Col. John Mitchell, downed Adm. Isoroku Yamamoto after one of the longest pinpoint interceptions in history. In May 1943, the 475th Fighter Group was created within the Southwest Pacific Theater as the only all-Lightning group. It quickly established a number of scoring records. Throughout the Pacific War, the Lightning proved itself as the premier Army fighter, as both Dick Bong and Tom McGuire proved. Flying only the P-38, Bong became America's ace of aces with forty kills, while McGuire got thirty-eight.

By 1943, the new P-38G was starting to enter service across the globe. With the P-38H came fully automatic supercharger controls for the 1,425hp Allison engines and automatic oil and coolant radiator doors. In the summer of 1943, the 449th and 459th Fighter Squadrons became the only two P-38 fighter units in the China-Burma-India Theater, operating at the end of a long and often forgotten supply line. The 318th Fighter Group flew the Lightning on long-range missions over the Pacific with the Seventh Air Force.

With victory in North Africa in May 1943, the Twelfth Air Force moved its P-38 groups to Tunisia, then through Sicily and Corsica. In early 1944, they were transferred to the strategic Fifteenth Air Force based at fields around Foggia, Italy. When the last of the P-38Js were being produced in mid-1944, the Lightning had not only dive flaps to prevent compressibility, but hydraulically boosted ailerons, improved cockpit heating, and improved deep chin intercoolers for the turbosuperchargers. Though the early-model P-38s had been more than successful in combat, the new models were the fighter everyone had envisioned, with virtually no limitations. Lightnings in the Mediterranean proved to be extremely effective, and they stayed in combat until the end.

In Europe, the 20th and 55th Fighter Groups took the P-38 into combat in October and November 1943 but lack of cockpit heat and supercharger problems plagued the aircraft well into 1944. By spring 1944, the P-38s of the 370th, 474th, and 367th Fighter Groups had been attached to the Ninth Air Force while the Eighth Air Force got the 7th Photo Group with F-5s. By the end of the war, all fighter units in Europe had transitioned to the P-47 and the P-51, except the 474th, which petitioned Ninth commander Gen. Pete Quesada to let them keep their beloved Lightnings. The final version, the P-38L, had 1,600hp engines. Seventy-five of these were converted into P-38M Night Lightning night fighters but they arrived in the Pacific too late to enter combat. The last of 10,038 Lightnings was rolled out in August 1945.

With the end of World War II, the P-38 Lightning, which had dominated much of the globe, was retired from service. The only reprieve from the smelter came in the form of the revived National Air Races, which lasted from 1946 through 1949, and aerial survey companies who found the F-5 an ideal mount. Lockheed test pilot Tony LeVier and a few others bought surplus P-38s and F-5s for $1,200 or so, then tried to soup them up for racing. Bill Lear, Jr., talked his father into loaning him the money to buy one for fun.

LeVier was by far the most successful Lightning racer, taking second in the 1946 Thompson Trophy Race at 370.1mph, then fifth in 1947. The most thrilling racing event for P-38 lovers was the 1947 Sohio Trophy Race, an all-Lightning event. LeVier took first among seven entrants in his slicked up, all-red P-38L-5.

In combat for just over three and a half years, the P-38 was one of the great American fighters of the war. Only a few remain flying out of the twenty-seven still in existence.

P-38 Lightning Photo Gallery

Elevator mass balances have been retrofitted to this YP-38, a supposed solution to tail flutter. Kelly Johnson was positive they were not needed, particularly since the buffeting was traced to wing-to-fuselage-pod-intersection turbulence, but the company refused to remove them. They became fixtures on every P-38 built, as did the large fairings fitted from pod to wing. Compare this fairingless YP with production Lightnings. *NASM Arnold Photo*

Maj. Signa Gilkey flies one of the thirteen service-test YP-38s. These sleek machines were the first to hit the mysterious phenomenon of compressibility; Gilkey was instrumental in figuring out how to deal with it. When the aircraft hit compressibility in a steep dive, its controls would lock up, making it virtually uncontrollable. No amount of pulling on the control wheel would budge the elevators; the natural reaction for the pilot was to go over the side. Gilkey, however, stayed with a YP in a prolonged dive and found that as it entered denser air he could pull it out using elevator trim. This led to extensive compressibility research and an eventual solution to the problem. *NASM Arnold Photo*

The first YP-38 on the Lockheed ramp at Burbank, September 1940, shows the exceptionally clean lines of Kelly Johnson's creation. Butt joined, flush riveted skin revealed Lockheed's obsession with getting every mile an hour they could out of the design, which had been extensively reworked to improve upon the ill-fated XP-38. *Lockheed Aircraft Corporation*

16

One of the 1st Fighter Group's P-38Ds with dummy guns during the Carolina Maneuvers of November 1941 (the red cross denoted the "enemy" Red Force). Though the early P-38s (there was no letter designation for the first production aircraft) and P-38Ds were not combat capable, they provided Army pilots with invaluable experience in handling this complex and imposing fighter. All of the early P-38s, through much of the E model run, had unpainted Curtiss Electric propellers. *NASM Arnold Photo*

Four P-38Ds on a practice mission, fitted with armament for a change. The early gun installation never incorporated the proposed 37mm Oldsmobile cannon, evident here by the faired-over hole in the center of the nose. Unlike future models, the early Lightnings, if guns were installed, had the four .50 calibers protruding evenly from the nose. Initial training was fraught with peril. If one engine failed on takeoff, the powerful torque of the other engine, no longer countered, could roll the big fighter over before the pilot could react. The exhaust residue from the turbosuperchargers is clearly evident on top of the booms. *NASM Groenhoff Photo*

Previous page
A P-38E over southern California irrigated fields during a sortie in mid-1942. The gun installation had now been standardized with staggered .50 caliber machine guns and a 20mm cannon. One of the most common marks of a well-used P-38 was the worn paint on the left wing running up from the trailing edge to the cockpit; this is where the pilot walked after stepping onto the wing from the folding ladder. *NASM Groenhoff Photo*

A new P-38E flies off the southern California coast just after the markings change order of May 12, 1942, which called for the removal of the red circle in the center of the national marking. The red circle still shows through the white star on the boom and the star and blue circle have not yet been repainted on the upper left wing. *NASM Groenhoff Photo*

This P-38E streams oil from its two Allison engines as it climbs for altitude. Another markings change took place in April 1942. Several manufacturers asked for permission to save paint and time in the panic-driven production effort by eliminating "US Army" below the wings of their products. By early May, aircraft were coming off the line without the label, but the marking change was never made official for aircraft already in service, so many retained the lettering. *NASM Arnold Photo*

One of the first batch of P-322-IIs, the last of the British reconversion project, at Shreveport, Louisiana, in January 1943. This non-turbosupercharged Lightning was used by the US Army Air Forces as a high-performance twin-engine trainer, keeping their RAF issue camouflage and serial numbers. *Fred E. Bamberger, Jr.*

The thirtieth P-38F built sits on the line in early 1942. At the time, the arrival of the futuristic P-38 at an Army air base was an event. The Lightning, more than any single Army type at the beginning of World War II, represented what the United States could do technically when the chips were down. The result was a great boost in morale and continual headlines for the P-38 and its pilots. *Fred E. Bamberger, Jr.*

A gunless RP-322 heads out over the Arizona landscape on a transition sortie. Though these "clapped" ex-RAF Lightnings had no high-altitude capability, they could really run on the deck, becoming the near perfect hot rod for new fighter pilots. With no gunnery training until the next phase of fighter lead-in, pilots had nothing to do but learn the fine points of flying the Lightning—in other words, joy ride. *USAF*

A flight of four P-38Es off the southern California coast, early 1942. Clearly, these fighters have seen a great deal of wear. Notice the worn paint from pilots walking up to the cockpit, deep exhaust trails from the turbos, matte paint polished to a sheen from wiping oil and scooting across the wings for maintenance, and oil seeping out at various places. Lockheed photographer Eric Miller took this shot from the open bomb bay of a Hudson. He recalled the Lightnings were being flown by sergeant pilots who later went to the 82nd Fighter Group as flight officers. The lead pilot chomps on a cigar. *Lockheed Aircraft Corp.*

The first fighter Lightnings to enter combat were P-38Es of the 54th Fighter Squadron, which began to fly sorties against the Japanese in the Aleutian Islands in August 1942. This 54th P-38E on jacks undergoes a periodic inspection and repair on the Eleventh Air Force base at Adak, late 1942. The rain, drizzle, cold, fog, and low clouds resulted in far more casualties than the enemy—for both sides. It was a tough theater of war in which to prove the Lightning. *US Army*

A group of 54th Fighter Squadron pilots walk out to their P-38Es before a mission from Adak, Aleutians, in late 1942. Though the clouds are low, the rain has stopped—good weather for this theater of war. At least it was cold all the time and pilots didn't have to worry about sweating in their heavy sheepskin jackets before reaching altitude. Long-range missions over the gray sea, which seemed to melt into the gray sky, were dangerous; pilots often flew into the water when there was no distinct horizon. *National Archives*

27

Capt. Harry W. Brown in the cockpit of *Sylvia*, his 475th Fighter Group Lightning, New Guinea, late 1943. On December 7, 1941, Brown was one of the few pilots to get airborne over Pearl Harbor in a P-36, downing two Japanese aircraft. He transitioned to Lightnings with the 9th Fighter Squadron, then to the 431st Squadron of the 475th in mid-1943. By the time he returned to the States, he had claimed five more victories. The 475th's P-38s were ridden hard and put away wet. *Dennis Glen Cooper*

A P-38H sits on the line at Williams Field, Arizona, late 1943. With the H model came a number of important improvements: automatic oil and coolant shutters, automatic turbosupercharger controls, and reduced intercooler leakage. The P-38H established the type as the premier fighter in both the Mediterranean and the Pacific theaters, giving pilots such as Tom Lynch, Dick Bong, Tom McGuire, Dixie Sloan, John Mitchell, Bob Westbrook, Danny Roberts, Charles MacDonald, Jerry Johnson, and Jay Robbins an impressive run of kills. *USAF*

As the war entered its third year, older versions of front-line aircraft were relegated to equipment tests and training. This Lightning, flying low over the Florida marshes, has smoke generators mounted on the pylons. The fighter has several different shades of olive drab applied as necessary to keep the metal covered, worn walkways up to the cockpit, and a replacement intercooler leading edge on the left wing. The national star and bar has not been painted back onto the new metal. Fresh olive drab paint has been applied to those areas receiving the most wear. *NASM Groenhoff Photo*

Capt. Willie Haning of the newly formed 475th Fighter Group at Ipswich, near Brisbane, Australia, August 1943. The 475th was the only new group in the Fifth Air Force to form outside the United States in order to save time in getting more P-38s into combat. The Lightning was Fifth Air Force commander Gen. George Kenney's favorite fighter. No one bothered to repaint this P-38 after it had been shipped halfway around the world—the Cosmoline and sealing tape hopelessly marred the pristine factory olive drab and gray paint. *Dennis Glen Cooper*

The first commanding officer of the 475th Fighter Group, Maj. George W. Prentice, stands in front of his P-38 in mid-1943. Prentice brought a wealth of experience to the new Lightning unit, having flown P-40s with the 49th Fighter Group, then commanded the 39th Fighter Squadron when they became the first to fly P-38s in the Southwest Pacific Area (SWPA). Kenney gave him virtual carte blanche to pull old hands from existing units, making the 475th, from the outset, a hot outfit. *Dennis Glen Cooper*

Sitting in a cockpit in the hot Pacific sun could be murderous, leading pilots to remove increasing amounts of clothing until some were flying in nothing more than shorts and G.I. shoes with a parachute strapped on. The extensive plexiglass of the Lightning canopy offered no respite at all, particularly since no part of it could be cracked open for air as in other fighters. If the windows on either side were rolled down, the resulting disturbed air hit the tail, creating an unnerving buffet. *Campbell Archives*

The Headhunters of the 80th Fighter Squadron weren't bragging out of turn with this sign at their headquarters in the Markham Valley of New Guinea when their score stood at 203 victories. The 80th received a total of four Distinguished Unit Citations for combat over Papua from July 1942 to January 1943, New Guinea from August to September 1943, New Britain in October and November 1943, and the Philippine Islands on December 26, 1944. Aces such as Jay T. Robbins (22 kills), George Welch (16 kills, four of which were gained over Pearl Harbor), Ed Cragg (15 kills), Cy Homer (15 kills), and Danny Roberts (15 kills) flew with the 80th. By the end of the war, the 80th had scored 224 of the 8th Fighter Group's 443 victories. *via Bob Rocker/Jack Fellows*

P-38s of the 39th Fighter Squadron and P-39s of the 41st Squadron, both attached to the 35th Fighter Group, sit alert at Dobodura, New Guinea, September 1943. Though the Bell P-39 Airacobra was far outclassed as a fighter, there were never enough Lightnings to replace the aging Bell products and the Curtiss P-40s that continued to fly combat. George Kenney's continual pleas for more P-38s had to compete with commanders in other theaters who wanted them. *via Jack Cook*

When Lockheed built the 5,000th Lightning, a P-38J, they celebrated by painting it a bright fire engine red with the name *Yippee* on the nose and under the wings. Lockheed chief test pilot

Milo Burcham flies *Yippee* over the southern California mountains on May 17, 1944. *Eric Miller/Lockheed Aircraft Corp.*

Lockheed chief test pilot Milo Burcham at the controls of the P-38J *Yippee*, the 5,000th Lightning built, May 17, 1944. Burcham was later killed during production testing of the P-80 Shooting Star jet fighter. (The author's father and P-38 gunnery instructor, Capt. Erv Ethell, was one of the pall bearers at Burcham's funeral.) Burcham was considered to be one of the finest test pilots of his era. *Lockheed Aircraft Corp.*

With telltale green spinners and individual aircraft letters on new P-38Js, the 80th Fighter Squadron heads out for takeoff at Nadzab in the Markham Valley of New Guinea. With the J model came virtual mastery of the air over every Japanese stronghold, including the oil fields at Balikpapan, Borneo, that were so vital to enemy fuel production. With aileron boost and improved turbosupercharging, this version of the P-38 was a formidable fighting machine. *via Bob Rocker/Jack Fellows*

An F-5B photo-recce bird is escorted by a P-38J fighter over southern California, fall 1943. The deeper chin under the fighter's engine is the result of moving the intercooler to that location from the wing leading edges, where they never worked consistently. Both aircraft still carry the rounded windshield with armor glass mounted behind inside the cockpit; this was later changed to a flat armor glass windshield. The F-5 carries Synthetic Haze Paint, used as an attempt to hide the airplane in the color of the sky. The scheme consisted of Sky Base Blue with a light shadow shading of Flight Blue, though it takes some real looking to see the differentiation. *Eric Miller/Lockheed Aircraft Corp.*

Capt. Tom McGuire's scoreboard on his P-38J *Pudgy III* at Hollandia, New Guinea. Kills 18 and 19 are freshly painted on, which dates the photo before June 16, 1944, when McGuire downed a Sonia and an Oscar to bring his score to 20. When McGuire was killed in January 1945, he had run his score up to 38 kills, making him second behind Dick Bong. McGuire was a fearless leader with an exceptional ability to fly the P-38. Wingmen said he wrung out his aircraft so hard that they flew "caddywampus" in a yaw after being "sprung." *Dennis Glen Cooper*

When the 318th Fighter Group received P-38s in place of its P-47s for long-range combat, the Lightnings came from several different units outside the Seventh Air Force. This P-38 sits on a coral strip shared by B-29s of the 73rd Bomb Wing, awaiting its next mission. Later P-51s would become the standard escort for Superfortresses hitting Japan. *73rd Bomb Wing Assn. via David W. Menard*

Satan's Angels, the 475th Fighter Group, had some of the most colorful Lightnings in the Pacific. Number 138 flew with the 431st Fighter Squadron, with the unit's Red Devil insignia on the radiator fairing and red trim on everything. The two red stripes on the tail signify the squadron commander, a device used in prewar units, then resurrected by several Pacific fighter groups. By war's end, the 431st had accounted for 225 of the group's 545 victories. *James G. Weir*

This imaginative piece of nose art, *Heady Hedy*, depicts a 44th Squadron, 18th Fighter Group P-38 pilot's dream of Hedy Lamar while stationed at Zamboanga, Mindanao, early 1945. Living in such a remote place, crews found their thoughts turn constantly to girls and food—or food and girls—the order never made much difference. *William Fowkes*

Bill Fowkes with his P-38J *Billy's Filly* at Zamboanga, Mindanao, in the first part of 1945. The 12th Fighter Squadron had moved across the Pacific, flying P-39s from Christmas Island and Efate, then P-38s form Guadalcanal and Treasury Island and on to Sansapor, New Guinea; Morotai; Lingayen, Luzon; San Jose, Mindoro; Palawan; Zamboanga; and Tacloban, Leyte. Flying with any group in the Pacific meant continually pulling up stakes to move to yet another series of tents until the war was finally over. *William Fowkes*

Control tower operators work with the 318th Fighter Group on Ie Shima. Most towers were open on sides, like this one, with a roof that gave only minimal protection from the elements. These guys had to stay at their post— even in driving rain—if aircraft were still airborne and overdue. In many ways, working in the control tower was a thankless job, particularly when more than one shot-up aircraft showed up, each declaring an emergency and asking for priority clearance. *Paul Thomas/Bob Rickard*

Hell's Angel was another 18th Fighter Group P-38J that flew out of Zamboanga in early 1945. The Lightning had an ideal nose for painting all manner of subjects, from dragons to cartoons, some quite elaborate. Often, the artist would remove the gun bay door so he could paint in the relative comfort (well, out of the sun anyway) of his tent. When finished, he'd bring the door back to be rehung. *William Fowkes*

A 318th Fighter Group P-38 on the line at Saipan in December 1944. The 318th received thirty-six well-used P-38s from the 21st Fighter Group in November 1944 and used them well into 1945. The "Lightning Provisional Squadron" did a good job of escort and long-range strike over Iwo Jima, Truk, and other distant targets until newer P-47Ns began arriving in early 1945 to carry on the job. *Paul Thomas/Bob Rickard*

A former 21st Fighter Group Lightning on the line at Saipan. Initially equipped with P-39s as defense for the Hawaiian Islands, the 21st received Lightnings but never used them in combat. In November 1944, thirty-six of their fighters were given to the 318th Fighter Group; in January 1945, the 21st was reequipped with P-51s. The 318th used the P-38s on some long-range escort missions and many came home single engine. *Russ Stauffer via Campbell Archives*

Lt. Howard Byram with his 19th Squadron, 318th Fighter Group P-38 on Saipan. The 318th transitioned from P-47Ds to Lightnings in order to give the Seventh Air Force a deeper striking capability against the Japanese. Pilots found themselves far out across the Pacific on missions that often lasted well beyond seven hours. Over such vast stretches of water, dead reckoning navigation—time and distance—was the only means of finding the way home. On one mission, Byram kept his P-38 going for 9.5 hours, limping back to Saipan from Iwo Jima, before his fuel supply was exhausted. He bailed out with only 25 miles to go and was picked up. The Pacific could be a lonely, forbidding place, particularly when separated and coming home alone. *Howard Byram*

Previous page
A new P-38J-10 cruises over the southern California mountains during a factory acceptance test flight in late 1943. This was the Lightning model that would establish the reputations of many aces and fighter groups, particularly in the Mediterranean and Pacific. Among the improvements for the pilot was a new control wheel with two pistol grips (the same type as on fighters with control sticks) and a flat, bullet-proof windshield. *Lockheed Aircraft Corp.*

At some point in P-38J-10 production from October to December 1943, Lockheed followed the US Army Air Forces directive to eliminate the olive drab and gray camouflage paint in favor of natural aluminum, as this example over California shows. Though pilots worried about their aircraft being more visible, the lack of paint made no difference in combat, other than saving several hundred pounds and possibly giving the pilot a bit more performance. *Eric Miller/Lockheed Aircraft Corp.*

As Jim Weir was undergoing combat transition training in June 1944 at Craig Field, Alabama, before heading for the Pacific, a veteran fighter pilot paid a visit to talk to the pilots and see how their training was going. Upon shutting down, 28 victory ace Dick Bong stepped out of this P-38 and spent some time with Weir and his fellow fledglings. After completing his second combat tour, Bong had been in the States since May 9. *James G. Weir*

Dick Bong taxies out after start-up at Craig Field, Alabama, June 1944, during his stateside visit. Though Bong considered himself "the lousiest shot in the Army Air Forces," he was certainly one of the most talented airplane handlers, able to maneuver up to point-blank range for his kills. Nevertheless, he wanted to learn to shoot properly so he reported to Foster Field, Matagorda, Texas, on July 7, 1944. By the time he graduated on August 6, he had put in over 50 hours of flying time. He returned to the Pacific for his third combat tour and destroyed another twelve Japanese aircraft by December to become America's top ace, with 40 kills. *James G. Weir*

Dick Bong's stateside P-38 at Craig Field, Alabama, during his visit in June 1944 with pilots on their way to the Pacific theater. Though Bong had to put up with a month's worth of bond speeches and publicity, he had come home to take his first serious gunnery training. Bong considered himself a poor marksman. "I am not a good shot," he said in an interview at the time. "I have to hit them either straight from behind or from straight ahead...or with a deflection of not more than ten degrees....I consider it a big accident when I hit anything with deflection shooting." *James G. Weir*

Jim Weir in the cockpit of his 19th Squadron, 318th Fighter Group P-38 on Saipan in late 1944. The 318th's veteran Thunderbolt pilots had racked up quite a record in combat since bringing their big single-engine fighters into combat off aircraft carriers. Transition to the Lightning was met with enthusiasm since it would give the group the range to reach the heavy action. After a few sorties, pilots were, on the whole, pleased to be flying the Lockheed product. *James G. Weir*

318th Fighter Group Lightnings peel off for landing at Saipan, late 1944. The World War II fan break was legendary. An entire squadron would come in toward the field in formation at low level, then break up into the landing pattern with little interval, creating the fan as fighters pitched up in sweeping turns all the way back down to the runway. Gear and flaps would be lowered at about the 180-degree point. The pilot would pull around and roll out just as he passed the end of the runway. Fighter pilots made a contest of seeing who could make the shortest elapsed time from pitch to touchdown. This was later outlawed, however, when pilots pulled too hard and stalled out, often killing themselves. *James G. Weir*

Lt. Jim Weir in front of Don Kane's *Killer's Diller*. Though the 318th Fighter Group painted the spinners of each Lightning red, the former 21st Group colors would often come through. In this photograph, the red is peeling off to reveal the original yellow. By February 1945 the Lightnings, which were hand-me-downs from the 21st to begin with, were deemed war weary and ordered transferred to Guam Air Depot. This left the 318th with their worn-out razorback P-47Ds and no worthwhile targets. After a much-resented forced rest, the group was assigned new P-47Ns and reentered combat in late April. *James G. Weir*

A well-dressed Fifteenth Air Force Lightning pilot, early 1944, wears a mixture of American and British equipment: a standard issue A-2 jacket and "pinks" (uniform pants), US Mae West and oxygen mask, and RAF helmet and goggles. The British helmet gave much better ear protection and radio clarity due to a deeper ear cup and better sealing around the ear. Being nonstandard items in the US Army Air Forces, the helmets were high on the list of items for trade. *USAF*

Gunless, all white, *Marjorie Ann*, was a P-38F used as a XV Fighter Command hack aircraft in June 1944. The red spinners were generic for all Fifteenth Air Force fighter groups. Stripped down, the old F was fast and fun to fly, though it finally got so tired and short of spare parts that it was pushed into the scrap heap. *Fred E. Bamberger, Jr.*

Post maintenance engine run, Foggia, sunset, Spring 1944. The right engine on No.13, 48th Squadron, 14th Fighter Group, is just starting to turn over as the crew chief holds the starter button down. The ground crew has pulled an extensive maintenance session in the mud and slime, with frostbitten fingers, and now they have to find out if No. 13 can be released for combat. There was little time to do such things as match the spinner color or even touch up the paint. *Ira Latour*

This Fifteenth Air Force P-38L Pathfinder at Cappodocino Airfield, Naples, June 1945, carries a large radar in the nose for ground mapping and lead bombing through an overcast. The Lightning was ideal for a number of modifications since the nose could hold just about anything. The Pathfinder, one of several Droop Snoot versions that could carry two people, had an external bomb load capacity of 4,000lb. A formation of P-38s dropping bombs aimed by a Droop Snoot could pack quite a wallop. *Fred E. Bamberger, Jr.*

Capt. Warren G. Campbell and his 94th Squadron, 1st Fighter Group P-38J *Old Rusty* at Foggia, Italy. The Lightning carried Campbell through forty-three missions in the Mediterranean Theater of Operations (MTO) where twin-engine reliability was as highly prized as in the Pacific. The 1st was one of the first Lightning groups into combat over Europe and North Africa after having flown across the Atlantic Ocean during Operation Bolero in June 1942. *Warren G. Campbell*

An F-5 of the 3rd Photo Group on short final to its base in Italy. The 3rd moved from England to the Mediterranean just after the invasion of North Africa in November 1942 under the command of the president's son, Col. Elliott Roosevelt, then proceeded to provide vital reconnaissance over Tunisia, Pantelleria, Sardinia, Sicily, Salerno, and Anzio before moving up to Italy and covering the invasion of Southern France. *Peter M. Bowers*

Seen through the Rotol prop blades of a 31st Fighter Group Spitfire VIII, a Free French recce Lightning of the Groupe de Reconnaissance II/33 lands at Pomigliano Airfield, Naples, early 1944. The "Photo Joe" did his job alone and unarmed; when someone failed to return from a mission, no one usually found out what happened. This was the case with the French author Antoine de Saint-Exupéry, lost July 31, 1944, while flying an F-5A with II/33 attached to the 3rd Photo Group. *William J. Skinner*

14th Fighter Group pilot Capt. William Palmer with his *Irene 5th* at Foggia, Italy, in 1944. The 14th, along with the 1st and 82nd Fighter Groups, stayed with their P-38s all through the war. Pilots found the fighter well-suited to combat in the Mediterranean and for long-range escort for the Fifteenth Air Force. Toward the end of the war, all three groups were given an increasing number of air-to-ground attack missions, which were far more dangerous than flying escort. *Norman W. Jackson*

Previous page
A 48th Fighter Squadron, 14th Group Lightning on short final at Triolo, Italy, 1944. The mud and grime on the P-38's wheels and booms is grim testimony to the conditions that dogged Army Air Force units in Italy. Combat did not wait for good weather or lack of mud, so the ground crews worked hard to keep their airplanes ready. *James M. Stitt, Jr.*

This was living, brother—at least at Foggia, Italy, in May 1944. This shack, built out of belly tank crates, belonged to Maj. Doc Crago, the 14th Fighter Group flight surgeon. He was particularly fortunate in having a shade tree to give him some respite from the Italian summer. With little in the way of basic accommodations, Twelfth and Fifteenth Air Force crews used every bit of raw material they could to improve things. *Norman W. Jackson*

In front of *Buzz* are pilot Capt. Norman W. Jackson (left) and crew chief Sgt. S. T. Mamore, 14th Fighter Group, 1944. Jackson had been one of the first replacement pilots to come to the 14th in North Africa in early 1943. He had a long tour of duty before heading back to the States as a P-38 instructor in late 1944. Since all

Fifteenth Air Force fighters had red spinners, about the only distinguishing mark 14th Lightnings had was the number on the side of the nose and on the radiator fairing; 131 was assigned to the 49th Fighter Squadron. At times, 14th aircraft had a stripe painted on the tail. *Norman W. Jackson*

The 82nd Fighter Group field at Foggia, Italy, 1945. The yellow-and-red control tower is hard to miss—I guess the tower operators didn't want any flat hatting fighter pilot to run into them. The 82nd was the third P-38 group to enter combat in the Mediterranean, flying their first combat mission on Christmas day 1942. By the time the war ended, the group had claimed 548 aircraft destroyed, another 88 probables, and 227 damaged. *Walter E. Zurney*

Next page
Sgt. Carl Belucher served as crew chief for Lt. Walt Zurney's 97th Squadron, 82nd Fighter Group Lightning *Taffy*. Zurney and Belucher shepherded *Taffy* through fifty combat missions. Zurney ended up flying twelve bombing missions in a Droop Snoot with a glass nose. As he should, Belucher reflects a great deal of pride in his airplane. *Walter E. Zurney*

2nd Lt. Richard E. Gadbury, one of two 97th Fighter Squadron bombardiers, in front of the 82nd Group Droop Snoot loaded for a bombing mission. These bombardiers had a unique job in flying with a fighter outfit since they were rated aircrew but not pilots. The idea was to lead a formation of bomb carrying P-38s with Gadbury or another of his colleagues in the front. All the P-38s dropped their bombs together on Gadbury's "bombs away." *Walter E. Zurney*

An 82nd Fighter Group Lightning with 150gal drop tanks loaded and ready for a mission. Ground crews would start working on their aircraft the minute the pilots shut them down. The crews would go through all the squawks noted by the pilot, rearm the guns, hang new drop tanks, and refuel. By the time the sun went down, the goal was to have the aircraft on the line, ready and in need of only a warm-up the next morning. *Walter E. Zurney*

95th Squadron, 82nd Fighter Group pilots (left to right) Lts. Del Ryland, Larry Peplinski, and Monty Powers, all shack mates at Foggia, in front of a squadron red tail, 1945. The other two squadrons carried different tail colors. The 96th was yellow or white and the 97th was black or blue, resulting in some colorful formations. *Ralph M. Powers, Jr.*

Lt. Monty Powers in the cockpit of his 95th Fighter Squadron Lightning at Foggia, 1945. The Lightning had a roomy cockpit, and pilots found that the control wheel allowed them to put quite a bit of muscle into maneuvering the large fighter. There were few unhappy P-38 pilots, particularly when the J and L models entered combat in 1944. *Ralph M. Powers, Jr.*

Working on a P-38 was a knuckle-busting proposition. The Lightning had two of everything (well, just about), compared to a single-engine fighter, and the cowlings were tight. It was not unusual for mechanics to have skinned, chapped, and bleeding hands. This 37th Squadron, 14th Fighter Group mechanic is already deep into his charge on a sunny afternoon at Triolo. *James M. Stitt, Jr.*

A 48th Fighter Squadron P-38J on takeoff at Triolo, Italy. The most dangerous part of flying the P-38 was the netherworld that existed between liftoff at 90 to 100mph and attaining best single-engine climb speed of 120mph. The pilot's manual was clear: "Be prepared to reduce power immediately to prevent uncontrollable yaw and roll in case of engine failure on takeoff...then apply power gradually and hold enough rudder to prevent the airplane from skidding." Pilots who did not pull the power back to stop the aircraft from rolling over paid for it with their lives. *James M. Stitt, Jr.*

May 1945, the war is over and Venice, Italy, never looked better, particularly from the cockpit of a P-38. While Lt. Glen Supp flew the piggyback fighter around the city, 37th Fighter Squadron engineering officer Capt. Jim Stitt took this shot from his cramped space behind the pilot's seat. With the war over, sight-seeing was the order of the day in every unit with airplanes, particularly for ground crews who had not seen much of the action. *James M. Stitt, Jr.*

A 37th Squadron, 14th Fighter Group crew chief
prepares his Lightning at Triolo, Italy, for the
day's mission. Though the Mediterranean was
supposed to be full of sun and sea, in the winter
it was cold and wet, requiring the heavy
sheepskin jackets pirated from bomber crews.
James M. Stitt, Jr.

This happy P-38 pilot, Lieutenant Honeycut of the 37th Fighter Squadron, is wearing his issue khakis instead of a flying suit. In the hot Mediterranean summer, rolled-up sleeves were standard. Though cotton was comfortable, once worn it stayed permanently creased until laundered, particularly in the sweat and heat. *James M. Stitt, Jr.*

In the blowing, swirling dust of Triolo, Italy, 14th Fighter Group Lightnings taxi and take off on a mission in 1944. Sand and grit were major enemies to units flying in the Mediterranean. Since the engine oil was not filtered by anything finer than the screen door mesh in the oil cuno and over the air intakes, dust passed straight into the engine to scour and grind away inside. Engine changes were regular occurrences. *James M. Stitt, Jr.*

Sunset at Triolo, Italy, winter 1944. As engineering officer Jim Stitt remembered, this 37th Fighter Squadron crew chief "will make the late mess—our guys got fed when they finished working and got to the mess hall." Getting the airplanes ready for the next day took precedence over every other activity, including sleep. *James M. Stitt, Jr.*

A 37th Fighter Squadron P-38J warms up in its revetment at Triolo, Italy, winter 1944, before taxiing out to the main runway for takeoff. The Foggia area was flat, ideal for missing obstructions during low approaches but was miserable when the wind picked up or the rain drove across the field or the snow blew through the tents and shacks. *James M. Stitt, Jr.*

A new 55th Fighter Group P-38G at Nuthampstead, England, December 1943. The 55th was the first Lightning unit to enter combat with the Eighth Air Force, flying their first mission on October 15, 1943. The group was also the first to fly over Berlin and by the end of the war, the 55th had destroyed more locomotives in strafing attacks than any other unit. *Air Force Museum*

The 38th Squadron, 55th Fighter Group propeller shop crew works on this P-38J at Nuthampstead. Left to right are T/Sgt. Harold Melby, Cpl. Merle Stivason, Sgt. Robert Sand, and S/Sgt. Kermit Riem. Though Curtiss Electric props were the source of much trouble, particularly in a wet climate like England, these men managed to rack up a record of consistent combat readiness for their P-38s, regardless of the conditions. *Robert T. Sand*

When 338th Squadron, 55th Fighter Group pilot Peter Dempsey went down to strafe a German airfield on May 21, 1944, he ran smack into a set of power lines while trying to fly under them and ended up bringing some wires home. Not only were the rudders locked up, as seen here, but the P-38 was riddled with machine gun fire as well as small- and large-bore flak. The windshield was solid black with oil and one engine was badly damaged, yet Dempsey brought it home to Wormingford. There is little doubt strafing was far more dangerous than air-to-air combat. *Robert T. Sand*

Sunset at Nuthampstead, England, the base of the 55th Fighter Group from September 16, 1943, to April 16, 1944. Personnel well remember the Tannoy loudspeakers that seemed to sprout from most areas of the field. They were extraordinarily clear, particularly when announcing Red Alerts of approaching bombers or—even more nerve racking—of V-1 buzz bombs, nicknamed Doodle Bugs. *Robert T. Sand*

The 55th Fighter Group lining up for takeoff at Wormingford, England, May 31, 1944. The sound of 200 idling engines running through turbos was never to be forgotten. "An all encompassing, but soft rumble" recalls Bob Sand. This day, the 55th was providing fighter escort for the Eighth Air Force heavies attacking marshalling yards and aircraft industry targets in Germany as well as targets in France and Belgium. *Robert T. Sand*

English fog was a constant for Eighth and Ninth Air Forces crews, almost as regular as sunrise. Though weather like this at Nuthampstead on December 26, 1943, would normally ground peacetime operations, the Eighth Air Force often flew, but not this day. The crew chiefs perform maintenance checks, something jumped at on non-mission days. Prop-shop mechanic Bob Sand recalls "sharp memories of this field in dense fog, pitch black night, and trying to tour my guard posts as sergeant of the guard. No headlights of course, and complete disorientation most of the time." *Robert T. Sand*

December 4, 1943. Crew chief Sgt. Red Fraleigh works on Lt. Jerry Brown's 55th Fighter Group Lightning (second from front) at Nuthampstead. Brown made a remarkable trip home single-engine and full of holes after being shot up by a German fighter, which was knocked off his tail by Captain Meyers. Working on a P-38 inside a hangar was a luxury; only the most damaged fighters were put inside. Usually, the crews had to work on them outside. *Robert T. Sand*

Three-quarters of the propeller crew at the line shack (if you can even call it a shack), Nuthampstead, 55th Fighter Group, 1943. Left to right are "Slim" Stivason, Harold Melby, and Kermit Riem. Since there were no permanent facilities on the flight line, crews built and assembled what cover or work spaces they could—at least enough to keep them out of direct rain or something to catch the heat of a potbellied coal stove. *Robert T. Sand*

Pilot Major Hancock and his ground crew, Technical Sergeant Gagnon and Sergeant Witmer, in a huddle before taking off for the first daylight mission to Berlin, "Big B," March 3, 1944. This mission was the one every pilot and crew had been waiting for—and the tension was more than tangible. As it turned out, bad weather forced the bombers back but the 55th Fighter Group didn't get the word and ended up over Berlin alone, the first Eighth Air Force aircraft to fly over the German capital since the war began. *Robert T. Sand*

Malcolm D. "Doc" Hughes' bent-up 7th Photo Group F-5 Lightning at Mt. Farm, England, April 20, 1944. Doc tried to break the low-level buzz job record and ended up flying into the intelligence building, raining white plaster dust on Pappy Doolittle and Walt Hickey, who ran from the building looking like ghosts and thinking they were under attack by a V-1. Doc feathered the left prop, seen here, and nursed his stricken bird to a landing. There were three gashes in the roof that group CO George Lawson ordered immediately repaired to keep Doc out of trouble but a 30-day grounding order was laid down. The group was glad when Doc got back in the air since, out of frustration, he took to driving a jeep like he flew. *Robert Astrella*

Previous page
Shark mouths seemed to have been painted on anything that flew, but the Lightning was ideal due to the shape of its two engine cowlings. This 7th Photo Group F-5C, *The Florida Gator,* went down over France on July 24, 1944, taking Lt. Edward W. Durst with it. Causes of recce aircraft losses were often difficult to ascertain since recce pilots flew alone, but the best guess was that Durst had passed out for lack of oxygen. *Robert Astrella*

Another veteran 7th Photo Group F-5 at Mt. Farm in 1944 shows some use. Though the PRU Blue paint leaps out at the viewer on the ground, in the air it was effective in camouflaging the aircraft. Recon pilots needed every bit of help they could get and the paint did help, but in the end, the pilot's survival depended on skill and a good measure of luck. *Robert Astrella*

This 7th Photo Group F-5 carries invasion
stripes on the lower half of booms and wings in
the latter half of 1944. Though the stripes were
supposed to keep Allied gunners from firing at
friendly aircraft, the paint didn't seem to stop it,
much to the frustration of photo pilots who
often had to drop down low over enemy lines to
get their pictures. *Robert Astrella*

Tough Kid, an F-5B, flew a long string of missions with the 7th Photo Group out of Mt. Farm through 1945. The camera ports on the front and side of the nose are evident, but rarely seen is the sighting scope retrofitted in front of the left windscreen. Photo Lightnings were the subject of many modifications, both at the factory and in the field, making each aircraft almost unique. The variety of camera ports and mounts alone was impressive. *Robert Astrella*

Previous page
Two 7th Photo Group F-5s line up for a formation takeoff at Mt. Farm in late 1944. Recce missions were normally single-ship. When a target needed broader coverage, however, two Lightnings would fly spread apart enough for the cameras in both aircraft to photograph a wider area. The fresh paint over repair and reworked spots points out just how much stock military paint would fade—in this case to a lighter blue. *Robert Astrella*

Little Jo, with the 7th Photo Group at Mt. Farm, reflects the official Army Air Forces' elimination of camouflage paint during the last year of the war. Initially, pilots were fearful that a natural metal surface would act like a mirror, reflecting sun to attract enemy pilots or showing up against the dark ground. As it turned out, the weight savings of several hundred pounds and less drag was a plus in combat. *Robert Astrella*

An F-5 taxies out for a mission at Mt. Farm in early 1945. The wet English weather turned the ground into impassable mud. Woe to the pilot who drifted even slightly off the taxiway since even full power would often not be enough to get him out. The pilot would have to get help, usually in the form of the mighty Cletrac "weasel," which seemed able to move just about anything through mud. *Robert Astrella*

Sgt. Julius Cooper, 38th Squadron, 55th Fighter Group painter puts some more paint on a newly arrived P-38J at Nuthampstead, April 11, 1944. When natural-metal aircraft first arrived in England, they were often painted in olive drab and gray camouflage or, if that could not be found, in RAF medium green and gray. These unprimed aircraft often shed their color. Before long, natural metal was accepted as normal and the practice of painting the aircraft at the bases stopped. *Robert T. Sand*

The long perimeter track at King's Cliffe, home of the 20th Fighter Group during its stay in England. The only readily available means of travel around this vast expanse was the ever-present English bicycle—particularly important when wanting to get from the flight line to the mess hall. Group supply records showed ordnance supply procured and issued over 3,000 bicycle parts—and this for only one fighter group; the order must have been enormous for a bomber group. *John W. Phegley*

The dispersal area, 55th Squadron, 20th Fighter Group, King's Cliffe, England, late June 1944. The group still carries the full set of invasion stripes, top and bottom. Drop tanks (150gal) and their crates litter the area behind the P-38J in the foreground, which was lost when 1st Lt. John Klink had to bail out over the English Channel (he was picked up). Though the grass was sectioned off and often reinforced with British wood interlocking plank, it remained a slippery, slimy work area. *John W. Phegley*

A 449th Fighter Squadron P-38J at Chengkung, China, January 1945. Lightnings were rare in the China-Burma-India Theater, so rare that only two individual squadrons were formed, then attached to a line fighter group as a fourth squadron. In the case of the 449th, they were attached initially to the 23rd Fighter Group from August to October 1943, then they were transferred to the 51st Fighter Group through the end of the war. Regardless of what you flew or what you did, this is what good accommodations were like in China. *Fred J. Poats*

Looking north at Ontario Army Air Base, just east of Los Angeles, early 1945. (Today, the mountains are still there but smog now obscures this once spectacular view.) Shown is one of the P-38Ls on the line for Lightning transition before the pilots headed for operational outfits. At this point in the war, many combat veterans served as instructors, passing on tips for surviving in hostile skies. *Norman W. Jackson*

Firefighting practice on a wrecked P-38L at Ontario, California, early 1945. With so many junior birdmen at one field trying to master the Lightning, accidents were inevitable, and the base firefighters tried to stay on top of what it took to save a pilot and put out the fire. *Norman W. Jackson*

A P-38L-5-VN, one of the 113 built by Consolidated-Vultee in Nashville, on short final at Ontario Army Air Base, California, in 1945. Not only are the flaps down, but the dive recovery flaps are extended along the bottom of each wing. This simple device allowed Lightning pilots to dive without worrying about compressibility and potential loss of control. *Norman W. Jackson*

Lightnings on the line in Alaska when the war up north was already over. In spite of the Japanese pullout from the Aleutians, the Army Air Forces maintained an air-defense capability in the region until the Japanese surrender. These P-38Ls are in excellent shape in spite of the often terrible weather. *R. Arnold via David W. Menard*

Lightning maintenance at Ontario Army Air Base, California, 1945. Southern California was ideal not only for year-round flying but for ground crews who needed to work on airplanes outside. Though the large hangar could clearly accommodate several aircraft, there were far more on the line around the field than would fit inside. *Norman W. Jackson*

The need for night fighters led to a contract for Lockheed to modify 75 P-38L-5s to P-38M-6 Night Lightnings with AN/APS-4 radar and a second seat for a radar observer. One proof of concept aircraft had already been modified at Hammer Field, Fresno, California, to serve as a prototype. Certainly the overall gloss black paint and red lettering caught the eye. *USAF*

When World War II ended, pilots found themselves in a sudden vacuum. The American war machine had produced almost 300,000 aircraft (among them 10,038 Lightnings), which were now massed all over the globe with nothing for them to do. Fighter pilots begged, borrowed, and stole what flying time they could in the rapid draw down, as Lt. Fred Poats, a 118th Tactical Reconnaissance Squadron P-51 pilot, is doing here at Hangchow, China, in October 1945. Fred gets in a little "exercise" with a 21st Photo Squadron F-5 to keep his skills up while waiting to be shipped back home. Unfortunately, most of the aircraft were so tired and, without wartime pressure to keep them in perfect shape, mechanical emergencies were common. *Fred J. Poats*

Pilot and radar observer climb into a P-38M Night Lightning. The observer had to be small of stature in order to fit into the tiny rear cockpit. The machine guns and 20mm cannon were fitted with anti-flash tubes at the front in order to preserve the pilot's night vision. Though the Night Lightning was shipped to the Pacific in strength, it arrived too late to enter combat. *USAF*

By 1946 the Army Air Forces had an obsolete fleet it didn't know how to get rid of. After all foreign customers had their pick, the P-38s were put up for civilian sale at $1,200 each; the rest were scrapped. These F-5s, P-38Ls, and P-38Ms at Clark Field, Philippines, in February 1946, await their fate under the shadow of Mt. Pinatubo. *via Glenn Horton*

Postwar use of Lightnings centered around two activities: air racing and photo surveying. The unfortunate result of this was the rapid demise of fighter Lightnings in favor of F-5s with good radios and cameras. Nevertheless, those few years of racing (up through 1949) gave the Lightning a colorful swan song. Shown is J. D. Reed's F-5, NX25Y, one of the most colorful racing Lightnings, emblazoned with sponsor Mobil's winged Pegasus. *NASM*

Charles Walling's 25Y had a number of modifications made to streamline it: slimmer fighter-style nose, earlier streamlined cowlings, repositioned carburetor intake, and clipped wings and outer horizontal stabilizers. Unfortunately, it wasn't a real winner against the Corsairs, Mustangs, and Airacobras. Though Walling placed second in the 1947 all-P-38 Sohio Race, he dropped out of the 1947 Thompson due to a balky fuel system. N25Y has survived to the present day, famous as the personal mount of Lefty Gardner. Lockheed test pilot Tony LeVier was by far the most successful Lightning racer, taking second and fifth respectively in the 1946 and 1947 Thompson and first in the 1947 Sohio with his blazing red P-38L-5. The aircraft ended up with Mark Hurd Aerial Surveys where it was destroyed in a crash in 1965. *Aaron King via A. Kevin Grantham*

Spartan Executive became one of the major postwar operators of aerial survey Lightnings, particularly those with Droop Snoot noses for an extra crew member who could operate cameras and line up the photo runs. This one is in particularly good condition as a working airplane, earning its keep and getting the attention it needs. *David W. Menard via Dick Phillips*

By the late 1950s and early 1960s, most warbirds had become so much junk, littering the ramps of airports around the United States. They were valued so low that few people could afford to put money into restoration and the aircraft became too expensive to operate for the return on aerial survey work. Some found their way into museums, like this F-5G at the Tallmantz facility, Orange County Airport, California, June 1966. The aircraft had been Bendix racer No.55 before going to the Honduran Air Force, then to Bob Bean in 1960, then to Tallmantz. David Tallichet ended up with it and put a fighter nose back on it. He flew it for awhile, then traded it to the Air Force Museum, which mounted it on a pole at McGuire Air Force Base, New Jersey, in 1981. *Jeff Ethell*

An Aero Service Corporation F-5G sits with flat tires next to a surplus Corsair in the western United States at about the time it was placed with the Pima County Air Museum by the Air Force Museum. The Aero Service Corporation, a Philadelphia-based company, put Lightnings to use through the end of the type's working career. Age and lack of parts, however, got the best of them and this is what happened. Many were saved, including this one, which was traded to the Musee de L'Air in Paris in May 1989. Unfortunately, it was destroyed a short time later in a disastrous fire that vaporized eighty-five other vintage aircraft. *David W. Menard via Dick Phillips*

Spartan Executive's survey operation spread across North America from Canada to Mexico, a mission particularly suited for the long-ranged Lightning. This Spartan F-5G was photographed from a sister Lightning doing its job over the vast Canadian lake country. Pilots quickly understood the problems faced by wartime bomber escort and photo pilots who sat for long hours in a cramped cockpit at altitude. This time there was only boredom without the momentary terror of combat. *Bob Bolivar via A. Kevin Grantham*

A Droop Snoot Spartan F-5G buzzes one of the Canadian airfields it operated from before the Lightnings were let go. Aerial photography was the last practical use of an airplane that had been designed before World War II. Although operators found it hard to replace as far as operational effectiveness, maintenance and age forced the aircraft out of everyday, on-the-ramp status. *Bob Bolivar via A. Kevin Grantham*

A forlorn Pacific Aerial Surveys, Seattle, two-seat F-5G at Santa Barbara Airport, California, July 1970. This Lightning had flown with Mark Hurd Aerial Surveys from 1953 before being sold to Pacific, who later sold it to Junior Burchinal. It ended up with Merrill Wein who painted it in 459th Fighter Squadron Twin Dragons markings before selling it to Charles Nichols' Yankee Air Corps at Chino. It then was sold to Doug Arnold who had it ferried across the Atlantic, then to Evergreen who brought it back to their facility in Marana, Arizona, where it has been restored by Bill Muszala and his crew. *Jeff Ethell*

Another Pacific Aerial Surveys F-5G at Santa Barbara, July 1970, when all service life had run out on these impressive aircraft. It would be many years before warbird market values climbed enough for buyers to invest in ground-up restorations. The Lightning was perhaps the most complex of wartime fighter aircraft to maintain, not to mention refurbish. *Jeff Ethell*

When Honduras finally let its P-38Ls go to surplus buyer Bob Bean in 1960, there was no great rush for the aircraft. Several sat rotting in the sun, like FAH504 (44-26961), on loan to Ed Maloney's Air Museum, Ontario, California, in October 1967. In 1969 ex-Lightning fighter pilot Larry Blumer purchased the aircraft and painted it in his markings as *Scrapiron IV* after restoration. In 1977 it ended up with John Deahl, who was killed in the crash of the Lightning some time later. The wreck ended up with Lester Friend. *David W. Menard via Dick Phillips*

Though many Lightnings were painted in wartime colors, only Darryl Greenamyer put the red colors of the 5,000th P-38 built, *Yippee*, on his personal airplane, seen here at Van Nuys, California, in June 1966, much the worse for wear. The F-5G had originally been given to Bolivia in the late 1940s under the Military Assistance Plan but never delivered. It was stored in Washington, D.C., until Jack Hardwick bought it in 1950. Ex-14th Fighter Group combat pilot Revis Sirmon bought the aircraft in 1969, built a fighter nose from scratch, and painted it in a fanciful camouflage scheme as N38LL. He flew it continually until a friend of his was killed in the aircraft in 1974. By that time, the warbird movement had picked up enough steam to see the P-38 as a rare find, and to this day it remains the most valuable of all ex-World War II fighters. *Jeff Ethell*

P-40 WARHAWK
in World War II Color

Jeffrey L. Ethell

Introduction

Hawks

Although the P-40 was deemed obsolete at the time of Japan's attack on Pearl Harbor, for the first year of the Pacific War it was the U.S. Army Air Force's most important fighter, if for no other reason than its availability. Its fame was sealed when Claire Chennault's American Volunteer Group (AVG), the Flying Tigers, successfully fought back the Japanese over China and Burma from December 1941 to July 1942 with their shark-mouthed fighters.

In October 1934, when Curtiss-Wright's Donovan R. Berlin began design work on the Hawk 75—later designated the P-36—he had no idea the airframe, basically unchanged, would live on in over 13,000 Tomahawks, Kittyhawks, and Warhawks (all versions of the P-40). By 1938, the P-36 had become the Army Air Corps' primary fighter, and Berlin got the Army's blessing to modify it by hanging an Allison V-1710 up front in place of the usual Pratt & Whitney R-1830. The result was the turbo-supercharged XP-37 which yielded 340 miles per hour at 20,000 feet—when the turbo worked. By December 1937 another thirteen YP-37s were ordered by the Army Air Corps

in hopes that the turbo's problems could be ironed out. Unfortunately, that was not to be.

Berlin tried a different tack. In standard trim, the 1710 made 1,090 horsepower at 10,000 feet. To up the power, Berlin asked Allison to step up the rpm of the 1710's single-stage mechanical supercharger. This V-1710-19 was installed in the tenth production P-36 airframe—modified with a belly scoop radiator—and flown for the first time on 14 October 1938. Dubbed the XP-40, it won the Army Air Corps' May 1939 fighter competition at Wright Field with a top speed of 365 miles per hour at 15,000 feet. The Army immediately ordered 524 examples. The $13 million tab was the largest fighter contract in American history.

In one of a number of top-level decisions indicative of what would later spell doom for the company, Curtiss-Wright management ordered Berlin to redesign the aircraft to mount the radiator under the nose. They thought it looked better this way, though it cost the aircraft speed. On 4 April 1940 test pilot Lloyd Childs flew the first production P-40, and by 1 June the Army began to take delivery of an aircraft that, from the firewall back, was essentially unchanged from its introduction in 1934. In September, the 8th Pursuit Group at Langley Field, Virginia, became the first AAC unit to convert to P-40s. The 20th Group at March Field, California, and the 31st Group at Selfridge Field, Michigan, soon followed suit.

Berlin was well aware of the aircraft's limitations. As the first P-40Bs were rolling off the Buffalo factory assembly lines in May 1941, Berlin was in England to question RAF pilots about the relative merits of British and German aircraft. After a glimpse of Rolls-Royce testing its new Merlin 60 engine, he quickly asked for this two-speed, two-stage supercharged, high-altitude engine for the P-40. Unfortunately, he was only able to swing the low-altitude Merlin 28 (for the P-40F and L), just slightly better than the 1,150-horse-power V-1710-39 being installed in P-40Es at the end of 1941. As a result, the P-40 was forever destined to be a low-altitude fighter. Berlin was so frustrated by Curtiss' lack of management and engineering foresight that he resigned at the end of December 1941, when only about 1,000 P-40s had been built, and went to work for General Motors.

Tomahawks

The first fifty-five Army Air Corps P-40Bs went overseas with the 15th and 18th Pursuit Groups at Wheeler Field, Hawaii. Another thirty-one went to the 20th Squadron, 24th Pursuit Group in the Philippines. The 33rd Pursuit Squadron was detached from the 8th Group to fly their P-40s to Iceland on 25 July 1941. The 35th Pursuit Squadron, 36th Group had gone to Puerto Rico the previous April, and the 16th Group had gone to Panama.

Through the P-40C, which first flew on 10 April 1941, all Hawk 81s (as the company called them) looked the same. A substantial number of these went to Britain's RAF as the Tomahawk Mk.I and II. By this time the Curtiss plant was running at maximum capacity with thirty production test pilots running from one P-40 to the next. To save time, new fighters were often flown out of the parking lot next to the plant instead of being trucked to the Buffalo Airport. The parking lot/landing strip was only 1,100 feet long and just slightly wider than a P-40's wingspan.

When the Japanese attacked Pearl Harbor on 7 December 1941 most of the P-36s and P-40s were lined up at Wheeler and Bellows Fields with empty fuel tanks and no ammunition, and the majority of them were destroyed in short order. Fortunately, almost unnoticed by the Japanese, the 47th Squadron had eight P-40Bs and six P-36As detached to the dirt strip at Haleiwa for gunnery training. Three 44th Squadron P-40Cs got airborne in the middle of the attack at Bellows, but all were shot down. Five pilots managed to get up to Haleiwa, under attack by a Val, and get two P-40s and five P-36s into the air. Though several kills were claimed against Japanese aircraft, by the end of the day there were only two P-40Cs, twenty-five P-40Bs, and sixteen P-36s still airworthy.

In the Philippines, the 24th Pursuit Group lost twenty-six P-40s, including some new E models, as well as the majority of its P-35s and obsolete P-26s. Most were hit on the ground at Clark and Iba Fields, though some pilots did get into the air; others were shot down on take-off.

In May 1941, the first RAF Tomahawks went into combat with No.250 Squadron in the Middle

East, followed by No.3 Squadron RAAF (Royal Australian Air Force), and No.2 Squadron SAAF (South African Air Force). By November, No.112 SquadronRAF and No.4 Squadron SAAF were flying Tomahawk IIBs over the Western Desert. Pilots were generally delighted with the rugged nature and excellent hitting power of the small fighter, finding few areas to complain about. Most aerial combat in the desert took place below 10,000 feet, making the Tomahawk an excellent dogfighter as well as a hard-hitting, close-air-support attack aircraft.

When the Flying Tigers took their 100 diverted ex-RAF Hawk 81A-2s (Tomahawk IIs) into combat in December 1941, they confirmed the British impression that the P-40 was an exceptional low-level fighter. Though they could not turn quite as tight as their opponents, mostly Ki.43 Hayabusas (even more maneuverable than the vaunted Zero), the Tigers found their Hawks could take on the opposition and win. High diving speed, rugged construction, armor protection, good firepower, and light controls made an excellent combination that enabled them to stop the Japanese in the air at a time when few others were able to do so. The Flying Tigers' signature shark mouths were copied straight off those painted on RAF No.112 Squadron's desert Tomahawks.

Kittyhawks

With the P-40D, the H87, came a major redesign including an enlarged radiator and oil cooler scoop, a new canopy, a fuselage shortened by six inches, shorter landing gear, removal of the fuselage guns, the addition of four .50 caliber guns in the wings, and a higher propeller thrust line.

When the P-40E flew for the first time in mid-1941 it had six .50s in the wings—standard armament from that point on. All subsequent P-40s stayed with the H87 designator; the British called them Kittyhawks, and the Army Air Forces eventually renamed its P-40s Warhawks.

Fortunately for the Army, there were enough P-40s on hand to keep throwing them into the breech against the seemingly unstoppable Japanese. The version most responsible for holding the fort in those dark days was the P-40E, built in larger numbers (2,320) than any other Hawk except the P-40N. Unfortunately, the E was more prone than previous models to swinging left on take-off, a problem wrestled with for some time. In a dive the controls got stiff while the aircraft tended to skid severely to the right even with full left rudder. The extended fuselages of later models solved these problems to a large degree.

Against overwhelming odds, Army pilots in the Philippines fought on. Most of the remaining P-40s were merged into a single Flying Detachment. Twenty Army pilots and their ground crews moved to Bataan Field with seven P-40Es and two P-40Bs and flew strafing, bombing, and recce missions from mid-January to early-April 1942. Though these brave men managed to get twelve kills and hold the Japanese invaders at bay to some degree, finally there was but a single P-40 left, this one assembled from the parts of the remaining aircraft. The day Bataan fell, the lone P-40E was flown out to northern Mindanao where four other P-40Es were still flying combat. When the islands were finally surrendered on 6 May 1942, the remnants of the Battling Bastards of Bataan's air force were blown up by the Americans.

Warhawks

The decimated 24th Pursuit (soon redesignated Fighter along with all other AAF fighter units) Group was reformed in Australia (with detachments sent to Java) in early 1942. The 24th was supplemented by the 49th Fighter Group which successfully defended northern Australia out of Darwin by shooting down numerous Japanese bombers and fighters. The 49th transferred to Port Moresby, New Guinea, in mid-1942 and flew Warhawks right up through the N model in 1943 before switching to P-38s. Another chopped-up unit, the 18th Fighter Group, got new P-40s and flew combat out of Guadalcanal with the E, F, M, and N models. In the Central Pacific, the mauled 15th Fighter Group flew an island-hopping campaign with a succession of models through the N until re-equipped with P-51s in 1944.

When the Flying Tigers were disbanded on 4 July 1942, the remnants became the China-based 23rd Fighter Group. The P-40E-equipped 51st Fighter Group formed in India, and by June 1943 two squadrons of the 80th Fighter Group were flying skull-nosed Warhawks out of Upper Assam, India. From their base in the Aleutians, the 11th and 18th Fighter Squadrons began fighting the Japanese in June 1942, while in the Mediterranean the 57th Fighter Group flew their first missions out of Palestine in August with P-40Fs and Ks.

Although the P-40F was powered by the Merlin 28, the Allison line kept going with the P-40K, which, like the F (after 699 were built), had 20 inches added to the fuselage midway through the production run to counter tail buffet. (As it turned out, the problem was an improperly redesigned scoop for the Merlin, something which fell on deaf ears despite Donovan Berlin's pleadings—yet another reason he left Curtiss-Wright.) Although at 10,000 pounds the K had the highest gross weight of any P-40 (the XP-40 weighed in at 6,870 pounds), the added horsepower of the modified Allison boosted top speed to 360 miles per hour.

During Operation Torch, the 8 November 1942 invasion of North Africa, the 33rd Fighter Group flew its P-40Fs off the carrier *Chenango* to Morocco while the 79th Group was delivered to Egypt by the *Ranger*. The 324th Fighter Group brought its Warhawks to the theater in December. The highlight of American P-40 operations in the Mediterranean took place on 18 April 1943, during the Palm Sunday Massacre. A formation of forty-seven Warhawks from the 57th and 324th Groups, covered by twelve RAF Spitfires, intercepted a mass formation of Ju 52s resupplying Rommel. In a short time fifty-eight Junkers transports were claimed destroyed along with eighteen Macchi 202 and Messerschmitt 109 escort fighters for the loss of one Spitfire and four P-40s.

April also saw both the P-40F-outfitted 325th Fighter Group and the all-black 99th Fighter Squadron (flying Warhawks handed down from other groups) enter combat from Africa. The 99th, in concert with three more squadrons, became the segregated 332nd Fighter Group. Both the 325th and the 332nd groups would later take their P-40s to Italy before re-equipping with P-47s.

The stripped-down "Gypsy Rose Lee" version of the Merlin-powered F was the L with four wing guns, less armor, lower fuel capacity, and some other things removed, to save about 250 pounds. A shortage of Merlin parts resulted in 300 Fs and Ls being re-engined with Allisons then relegated to training command as P-40Rs.

Out of the L and its Allison-powered M brother came the most-produced Warhawk, the P-40N, a direct approach to increasing performance by reducing gross weight to 8,850 pounds. With a 1,200-horsepower V-1710-81, the N squeaked to 378 miles per hour, which by 1943 standards was well below other first-line types.

In spite of its lesser performance, the P-40 continued to be used right up to the end of the war by such diverse combat units as the AAF and RAF Commonwealth forces of Australia, Canada, South Africa, and New Zealand, as well as the air forces of Russia, China, and France. The last P-40 of 13,737 built, a P-40N-40-CU (44-47964), rolled off the line on 30 November 1944. To give an idea of what mass production could do, the P-40B cost $60,562 in 1941 while the P-40N of 1944 cost $44,892. The homefront American industrial worker performed a production miracle that won World War II.

The last version, the XP-40Q, had a bubble canopy and a four-bladed propeller. Created from a P-40K-1, it was far too late, arriving at Wright Field in early 1945 for evaluation. With a high-altitude Allison V-1710-121 producing 1,425 horsepower, it finally got up there with the big boys,

able to top out at 422 miles per hour with a service ceiling of 39,000 feet.

Universally, P-40 pilots loved their airplane, many choosing to continue flying it even when other more powerful types were offered. Bill Stubbs, who flew in the Mediterranean, confirmed that "the P-40 could outdive about anything, and indicated airspeeds of 600 miles per hour were not unheard of. However, it did want to pull to the right in a dive, and when it was desirable to hold it straight, as for dive bombing, it needed a lot of left rudder pressure—so much so that it was alleged that one could always spot a P-40 pilot by the over-developed muscles in his left leg."

R. T. Smith, one of the AVG's aces, thought the Curtiss fighter served the Flying Tigers well. "I really loved that old P-40. It was reliable, could take a helluva beating and still get back home, and if you pointed the damn thing in the right direction you could get pretty good results. I was mad as hell when another guy cracked up my old No. 77 while I was on a ferry trip to Africa. It gets to be quite a personal feeling for your own airplane, the one with your name painted up near the cockpit, and none of the others ever feel quite the same. Sorta like members of the opposite sex, maybe: they're all built more or less identical, but . . . "

P–40 Warhawk Photo Gallery

The family resemblance between this Wright Field Materiel Division Curtiss P-36 and the P-40 is unmistakable. The tenth production P-36 became the XP-40 with the only major change being an Allison V-1710 in place of the Pratt & Whitney R-1830. The result was near instant obsolescence when compared to the fighters being built in Europe and Japan. *NASM Arnold Collection via Stan Piet*

Previous page
New P-36Cs of the 36th Pursuit Group on the line at Langley Field, Virginia. The P-36 was a wonderful aircraft to fly according to its pilots—a real sports car with light controls and excellent maneuverability. Unfortunately its top speed of 323 miles per hour (the P-36A only managed 300 miles per hour) was far below modern standards, a reflection on the state of an American aircraft industry struggling through the Depression and isolationism. *USAF via Stan Piet*

Above
These 27th Squadron, 1st Pursuit Group P-36Cs sit ready for the National Air Races, September 1939. The garish camouflage was created specifically to make an Army splash at the races, and it was never used in the maneuvers or wargames for which such schemes were normally slated. The 27th Squadron badge is just visible behind the wingtip of No.69. No two of the schemes were alike. *USAF*

In early 1941, the aspirations for modern fighters in the U.S. Army Air Corps were pinned on these four aircraft. From top to bottom are the second YP-38 Lightning, a production Bell P-39C Airacobra, a production P-40, and a Republic YP-43 Lancer. The P-38 was the best of the lot. The lengthened tailwheel strut on the P-40 is fixed down as a stopgap measure to improve the fighter's ground looping characteristics. *NASM Arnold Collection*

Next page
The XP-40 in its final form (the radiator was moved from the belly to the front, much to designer Don Berlin's disgust) without armor or armament was assigned to the Air Corps Materiel Division, Wright Field, Ohio. The stripped "hot rod" prototype had excellent performance when compared to heavier service models. *NASM Arnold Collection*

A 33rd Squadron, 8th Pursuit Group P-40 at Langley
Field, Virginia, 1941, just after the group became the
first in the Air Corps to be equipped with the type.
It was standard practice to paint the squadron emblem
on the side of each fighter, adding some much-needed
color to an otherwise drab aircraft. Other flights in the
squadron had yellow and white nose markings.
USAF via Stan Piet

Next page
Time for a flight marking change as the mechanic
oversprays what used to be a red nosed (and before that
blue) Tomahawk. Markings were never pristine when
viewed up close—there was a job to be done and
ground crew did not have a great deal of time to make
things look perfect. The chamois-padded, rubber ear
headset was typical equipment for the day, resulting in
extensive hearing loss. The rubber never seemed to
enclose the ears as much as smash them flat. The
headsets were good, however, for producing that fifty
mission crush look on one's hat. *USAF*

Previous page

A 35th Squadron, 8th Pursuit Group pilot climbs from P-40-CU serial number 39-189 at Mitchel Field, Long Island. It wouldn't take long to go deaf wearing only this regulation Army issue headset, and the A-2 jacket provided absolutely no warmth, being good for little more than show. The first production P-40s did not have letter suffix model designations, something that didn't come along until the P-40B; this was the case on all other Army aircraft as well. Lack of model designations led to a fair amount of confusion, so the system was later changed to give the first production runs of new aircraft an "A model" suffix. *NASM Arnold Collection via Stan Piet*

Mechanics hover around an early P-40-CU at Mitchel Field. The fighter's tightly cowled engine proved to be a knuckle-busting nightmare, particularly in the harsh conditions of combat. The closer the cowling, the higher the speed, but when a mechanic had to shove his bare hands up into a blistering hot engine compartment, he wasn't that impressed by airspeed. Can you imagine doing this with two Allisons on the same aircraft? The number of men here is about right—it took a ground crew long hours of work each day to keep a World War II fighter airworthy. *NASM Arnold Collection via Stan Piet*

Standard 1941 high-altitude flying equipment is
modeled by this 8th Pursuit Group pilot at Mitchel
Field. The bladder oxygen mask would later give way
to diluter-demand systems, but the helmet, goggles, and
shearling leather suit and boots would remain standard,
particularly for bomber crews, through most of the war
until replaced by electrically heated garments. These
suits were particularly bulky in the tight confines of a
fighter cockpit and many pilots elected to wear multiple
layers of long underwear and wool clothing instead.
The last thing a pilot wanted in combat was the
inability to move quickly from side to side and look
directly to the rear. *NASM Arnold Collection via
Stan Piet*

A flight of unarmed early-production P-40-CUs climbs
out on a training flight in late-1940. Each of the Hawk
pilots has opened the radiator gills under the rear
section of the nose to get increased cooling of the
Prestone glycol/water mixture. From the P-40's first
days, overheating was a constant problem, particularly
when taxiing. Much of the problem had to do with the
radiator subcontractors, as some manufacturers built
units that seemed to have no problem at all, while
others built radiators that caused the coolant to boil
over. Curtiss pilots watched their engine temperature
gauges more than any other single thing in the cockpit.
NASM Groenhoff Collection

Army pilots do a little staged preflight planning for the photographer with their new P-40Cs in the summer of 1941. Just visible on the wing leading edges are the cutouts for two .30 caliber guns per side—standard armament, along with the nose-mounted .50s, for the C. The B had only one .30 caliber gun per wing, while the P-40 (no letter suffix), had only the nose-mounted .50s. From a distance the differences in these early Hawk 81s are hard to distinguish, a problem compounded when a full complement of guns was not installed. *NASM Groenhoff Collection*

The calm before the storm. A 20th Pursuit Squadron P-40B cruises over Clark Field, Philippines, in the summer of 1941. Ill-prepared for war, the Army Air Forces had a hard time fielding modern equipment, let alone enough of it. Knowing what would happen if war started, 20th Squadron pilot Max Louk wrote home in November that they were "doomed at the start." There would never be another summer quite as idyllic as that year in the Philippines, a Pacific paradise for the prewar Army. *Fred Roberts via William H. Bartsch*

The AVG line at Kunming, early 1942, shows the Fleet Finch trainer used as a hack by the pilots and the fine dirt area which caused constant trouble with the Allison engines. By May the Hawks were so worn out that only small formations could be put up at any one time. The more success Chennault's boys had, the more difficult it seemed to be to get U.S. Army support, particularly in the form of replacement aircraft. During their entire time in combat, the Flying Tigers received a total of thirty P-40Es which Chennault had to sweet-talk the AAF powers-that-be into letting him divert from their original destination (Java). *R. T. Smith*

American Volunteer Group ace R. T. Smith sits in the cockpit of Hawk 81A-2 No.40 at Kunming, China, in early 1942. Claire Chennault's Flying Tigers made the P-40 famous by giving the Japanese a real trouncing in the first six months of the war. Basically export versions of the P-40C, the AVG's diverted RAF Tomahawk IIs were emblazoned with Walt Disney's flying tiger decal, which had been created and shipped to Chennault free of charge. For preservation, each of the decals was shellacked, clearly evident on No.40. *R. T. Smith*

122

Hell's Angels, Third Squadron, Flying Tigers on patrol over the Burma/China border, mid-morning, 28 May 1942. In the lead is Hell's Angels Squadron Leader Arvid "Oley" Olson flying Chuck Older's No.68 as the six fighters (including R. T. Smith's No.77 from which this shot was taken) head northeast near the Salween River toward Pao Shan to intercept a possible Japanese bombing raid. In echelon behind Olson are Bill Reed, Tom Haywood, Bob Prescott, and Ken Jernstedt. After about an hour with no enemy contact they headed back to Yunnanyi to refuel, then home to Kunming. *R. T. Smith*

This P-40-CU serial number 39-184 was flown out of Luke Field, Arizona, for fighter transition training. As with all the other early "plain vanilla" P-40s they lacked self-sealing fuel tanks, armor, and guns making them light and fun to fly, though they did get long in the tooth by 1942 when this photo was taken. In late 1941, when the author's father, Erv Ethell, was flying one of these P-40s at Luke during the last part of Advanced Flight Training, he heard a tremendous banging as he was cruising along. Sure the fighter was coming apart in the air, he slid the canopy back, unstrapped and started to climb out on the wing to jump when he noticed the sandpaper-type wingwalk had come unglued and was flapping madly against the metal skin. He sheepishly got back in and turned for Luke. *USAF via Stan Piet*

Previous page
The two aircraft types used for Advanced Flight
Training at Luke Field in 1941 and 1942—a P-40-CU
and an AT-6C—cruise over the Arizona desert. A
select number of promising Advanced students were
selected from their class to fly the last ten hours of their
training in the P-40, which usually meant they were
assured of getting fighters upon receiving their wings.
Moving from the Texan to the Hawk was breathtaking,
the fulfillment of a dream to be an Army fighter pilot.
USAF via Stan Piet

This new P-40D over Buffalo represents the first major
reconfiguration in the fighter's shape. The company
changed its internal designation from Hawk 81 to
Hawk 87. Though the British changed their name for
the P-40 from Tomahawk to Kittyhawk with this
version, the latter did not really take with U.S. Army
versions, which were called, for the most part,
Warhawks from this point on. The new Allison engine
had an external reduction gear (earlier versions had
used an internal reduction gear) which made the
powerplant shorter and resulted in a raised thrust line,
which in turn allowed the landing gear to be shortened.
The radiator was enlarged and moved farther forward,
and the guns in the nose were removed. *NASM Arnold
Collection*

When the P-40E came along it was smack in the middle of the strong British buy of Kittyhawks. This Kittyhawk IA had some stars slapped on it and was sold to the Air Corps as a P-40E complete with its standard RAF paint scheme, which was labeled medium green and sand with light blue undersurfaces. In the middle of the E production run Pearl Harbor was attacked and this model became the Army fighter that held the fort for the first year of war. *NASM Groenhoff Collection*

Next page
Three of Curtiss-Wright's most experienced test pilots, Byron Glover, C-W Chief Test Pilot H. Lloyd Childs, and Russell Thaw, with a new Merlin-powered P-40F at the Kenmore Plant in Buffalo. These men are wearing the adapted hard car racing helmets common with many company test pilots across the country—a trend that would eventually lead to hard aviation helmets becoming standard. The Merlin-engined P-40s were easy to recognize as they had no carburetor air scoop atop the cowling. At its height, Curtiss-Wright at Buffalo kept thirty production test pilots on the run to keep the flow of aircraft unhindered. *NASM Arnold Collection via Stan Piet*

A 343rd Fighter Group Warhawk taxies off the runway at Longview Field, Adak, Aleutian Islands, in late 1942. Blowing snow was far preferable to ice or mud, though anything but dry conditions could cause a pilot to lose control of his aircraft. As it was, the P-40 was a ground looper—it didn't need any help. The P-38s on the line across the field belong to the 54th Fighter Squadron, the first unit to take the Lightning fighter into combat the previous September. *National Archives*

Combat duty in the Aleutian Islands was only slightly better than miserable, even on a good day—which meant a day when it wasn't snowing, sleeting, or covering everything with a sheet of ice. This 343rd Fighter Group flight line at Adak on 9 April 1943 gives a good idea of what it was like. The ice and snow has been cleared off the pierced steel plank (PSP) where aircraft have to move or park, and the fuel truck is the mighty Cletrac, which could move through just about anything, whether mud, snow, or ice. The men and women of the 11th Air Force in the Aleutians were all but forgotten as the rest of the war seemed to overshadow them. *National Archives*

Bengal Tigers of the 11th Fighter Squadron parked at Adak, Aleutian Islands in mid-1943. Commanded by Col. John "Jack" Chennault, son of Gen. Claire Chennault, the 11th's P-40s were painted in a variation on the theme made so famous by the Flying Tigers. Pierced steel plank was an absolute necessity for operations in Alaska...otherwise the aircraft would have bogged down in the constant mud. *National Archives*

A Cletrac tows an 11th Fighter Squadron Bengal Tiger Warhawk down the 28th Composite Group line at Adak in the spring of 1943. The lower cowling has been replaced and the tiger face has yet to be repainted, though a squadron emblem remains. Fighter cockpits were notoriously cold with seemingly little thought given to ducting some of the Allison's great heat back to the pilot. In the Aleutians it was even worse because pilots started out cold from long nights in ill-equipped tents. Getting warm was a major pastime. *Via David W. Menard*

One of the maintenance areas at Adak, late 1942—rarely was anything done inside. The 28th Composite Group had a wide variety of aircraft under its wing since there were rarely enough squadrons of a single type to create a specialized outfit. As a result, mechanics had to work on fighters, bombers, and liaison types interchangeably. At least the Allison engine was common to the P-38, -39, and -40. From he looks of the propellers on the Warhawks to the left, the first was probably bellied in while the second had a prop strike, probably from nosing over enough to tip the prop. *National Archives*

P-40Fs of the 33rd Fighter Group are officially presented to the French GC II/5 Groupe Lafayette, or Lafayette Escradrille, at Casablanca, 9 January 1943. Though the 33rd could not afford to lose any of its Warhawks, Allied planners believed it important to re-equip this French unit quickly since it had been a Vichy unit fighting against the Allies during the invasion of North Africa. As soon as the French took delivery of twenty-five P-40Fs on 25 November 1942, two weeks after the invasion, two of the pilots defected to German-occupied southern France with their new Hawk fighters. Nevertheless, the group fought with the Allies, eventually re-equipping with P-40Ls, then P-47Ds. *USAF*

Yessir, living in the Aleutians was sure great fun. Though all theaters of war had problems with mud, when it was frozen it seemed to be about as bad as it could get. The Jeeps and the Dodge Command Car here were about the only method of transportation, aside from the Cletrac, that could manage the muck, but even these were often left sitting in favor of walking. Flying airplanes was the least of one's worries. *National Archives*

The famous World War 1 Sioux Indian head, Lafayette Escadrille, insignia adorns the side of this Free French GC II/5 P-40F at Casablanca on 9 January 1943. The French Armee de l'Air Catholic priest, who also wears a pilot's brevet and decorations, had blessed the aircraft before taking time to talk to these AAF pilots. The Groupe, which had flown Hawk 75A-4s against the Allies as a Vichy unit, went on to fight with distinction in the Tunisian campaign, once again flying the flag of the famous American pilots who had fought so well as volunteers twenty-five years earlier. *USAF via Stan Piet*

Charles "Jazz" Jaslow with Phil Cochran's 57th Fighter Group P-40E at Bradley Field, Connecticut, in May 1942 just before the unit shipped out for Palestine. Cochran would later become famous for his combat flying in the China-Burma-India Theater as head of the 1st Air Commando Group. Cartoonist Milton Caniff had much to do with this by creating his thinly veiled "Terry and the Pirates" character Flip Corkin. The Group, along with all other AAF fighter units, had been redesignated from "pursuit" to "fighter" on 15 May 1942. *Charles Jaslow*

Though squadron emblems were normal decoration on Army fighters through 1942, the practice, on the whole, was dropped by almost all units except the 57th Fighter Group, which carried the decorations through their combat days in the P-40 and P-47, then into the postwar era with jets. Jazz Jaslow leans on the 65th Squadron CO's P-40E at Bradley Field, Connecticut, May 1942. The 56th's fighting gamecock, with the chip of wood on his right shoulder, made a great piece of art. *Charles Jaslow*

These pilots of B Flight, 87th Squadron, 79th Fighter Group at Rentschler Field, Connecticut, were transferred intact from the 65th Squadron, 57th Fighter Group when the 57th was moved overseas in early July 1942. Around the 87th Squadron "Skeeters" emblem are Scotty Rogers, Frank Huff, James Hundley, Leo Berinati, Ed Holston, John Dzamba, Charles Jaslow, and Red Crossley. By November these men would be in combat in Egypt. *Charles Jaslow*

Lt. Jazz Jaslow (right) with his crew chief R. Randall and their 87th Squadron, 79th Fighter Group P-40F X81 *Sweet Bets*. Jaslow drew Dopey on the rudder using crayons, the only medium he could find, along with the phrase "Passionate Dwarf." Jaslow picked the Disney character because he was considered the small fry of the squadron. Rudder art was common on North African Warhawks. *Charles Jaslow*

Jazz Jaslow with the other end of his 87th Fighter Squadron P-40F *Sweet Bets*, which featured an enlarged version (compared to the previous stateside shot) of the "Skeeters" squadron insignia on the nose. The telltale lack of a carburetor air scoop atop the cowling was an easy way to spot all Merlin-engined P-40s, including the Ls. The RAF Sand and Stone/Azure Blue camouflage was an improvement over solid AAF Olive Drab and Gray in the barren wastes of the Western Desert. *Charles Jaslow*

Pilots and Warhawks, 87th Fighter Squadron, 79th Fighter Group, ready to "crank" at Castel Benito Airdrome, Tripoli, Libya, March 1943. The constant dust/mud of North Africa was rough on both planes and pilots—it seemed to be in the food, the oil, the bedding, the eyes, everything. The only respite was to get airborne. Sitting alert in the hot sun was close to insanity at times. *Charles Jaslow*

The 87th Fighter Squadron spread out across the field at Houaria Landing Ground at the tip of Cape Bon, Tunisia, in the spring of 1943. This bit of Africa which stuck out into the Mediterranean was a good spot for the P-40s. Any Luftwaffe incursions from Sicily and Italy could be intercepted rapidly, particularly the formations of lumbering, near defenseless Ju 52s carrying troops and supplies to Rommel. *Charles Jaslow*

The Me 109 kill on Jazz Jaslow's P-40F reflect the results of a successful fight on 2 April 1943 near Wadi Akarit. From a certain point in the F model's production run forward, with the exception of the K and some other later airframes, Curtiss fitted an ice window to the left front windshield. No one ever seemed to know why, since very few P-40 pilots fought under conditions where ice would be a problem; besides, the canopy could be opened in flight at all speeds. All the ice window really seemed to do was further reduce the already restricted visibility. *Charles Jaslow*

Out to see the sights, 87th Fighter Squadron pilots.
Charles Jaslow

This German Kübelwagen, the enemy's Volkswagen-built version of the Jeep, was requisitioned in good working order by Jazz Jaslow in the desert so he could learn to drive! The 87th Fighter Squadron combat pilot was flying Warhawks but had never been taught the intricacies of the automobile. By the time the squadron moved on he had learned, thanks to the Germans.
Charles Jaslow

The remains of Scotty Rogers' P-40F after the 87th Squadron's first night landing in the desert. Unable to see, he taxiied into a 55-gallon gas drum which promptly blew up. So much for one relatively new Warhawk. Fortunately the pilot walked away.
Charles Jaslow

Pilot Jazz Jaslow and his 87th Fighter Squadron crew chief, R. Randall, on Jaslow's P-40F, *Sweet Bets,* spring 1943, proudly frame Jaslow's 2 April 1943 Me 109 kill. The 87th, a part of the 79th Fighter Group, was in Egypt by November 1942, then fought through Libya, Tunisia, Malta, Sicily, and Italy, in addition to a short spell in southern France. Before it was all over, the squadron received two Distinguished Unit Citations, one for combat over North Africa and Sicily from March through August 1943 and the other for action over Italy 16–20 April 1945. *Charles Jaslow*

Spread across the field at Asmara, Eritrea, are new P-40s, ready for test flying over the Abyssinian mountains before heading off to combat. The woodie station wagon, a real find in this barren wasteland, had been commandeered by the Army for use on the field. Some of the 79th Fighter Group's pilots had to fly down to this field to pick up spare aircraft that had been shipped over in crates on freighters, hauled up to the mountains 7,000 feet above sea level, assembled , test flown, and then delivered to the fighter squadrons in the field. *Charles Jaslow*

A 33rd Fighter Group P-40E sits ready at Martin Field, Baltimore, Maryland, in early 1942 as the unit works up for combat. The markings below the wings still include the red-centered star and U.S. ARMY. Both were eliminated in short order, the former because of confusion between it and the Japanese Hinomaru rising sun. By the end of the year, the 33rd would be in combat over North Africa. *J. P. Crowder via Dorothy Helen Crowder*

June 1942: A 33rd Fighter Group P-40F Warhawk over Maryland during lead-in combat training. The red-centered stars are gone, as is the large lettering under the wings. This is the Merlin-engined model the group would also take into combat over the desert, a fortunate happenstance which was often not the case. Many groups would train in one type, then end up with an entirely different aircraft in the combat zone.
J. P. Crowder via Dorothy Helen Crowder

A 33rd Fighter Group P-40F on the Harrisburg, Pennsylvania, ramp of the 103rd Observation Squadron, National Guard. A brand new PT-19, on a test flight from the Fairchild factory at Hagerstown, Maryland, shares the space. The Douglas O-46A was based at the field with the 103rd. Before heading overseas, fighter pilots enjoyed the best of times with the ability to take their aircraft just about anywhere to visit family or buzz everything in sight. It was the world's best flying club, but that would change in a heartbeat once overseas. *J. P. Crowder via Dorothy Helen Crowder*

Next page
A steel helmet was standard issue for fighter pilots in North Africa since they lived out in the open, in tents or foxholes. John P. "Jeep" Crowder stands in front of his 59th Squadron, 33rd Fighter Group P-40F at Thelepte, Tunisia, early-1943. *J. P. Crowder via Dorothy Helen Crowder*

Sunset at Thelepte in the Tunisian desert, January 1943. North Africa was a torture chamber of temperature changes—hot and windy in the daytime, freezing and pitch black at night. Getting warm seemed an impossible task with the standard-issue Army blankets and tents. Some crews preferred to sleep in their aircraft, a real task in a fighter. *J. P. Crowder via Dorothy Helen Crowder*

The sum total of 59th Fighter Squadron operations at Thelepte, Tunisia, January 1943—nothing more, nothing less than a hole in the ground. Though the ground was baked hard, seemingly impervious to the Army issue spade, it was worth the effort to get out of the wind. Additionally, the holes provided air raid protection from anything but a direct hit. *J. P. Crowder via Dorothy Helen Crowder*

An extended fuselage P-40L Warhawk of the 59th Squadron, 33rd Fighter Group, cruises over North Africa, early-1943. The group had flown its fighters off the aircraft carrier USS *Chenango* as a part of Operation Torch the previous November, then set up bare-base operations in French Morocco. The large American flag painted on the side was one of many attempts to identify American planes to the Vichy French defenders, implying the invasion was an all-American operation. The French had little love for the British so the Allied strategy was to play down British participation. *J. P. Crowder via Dorothy Helen Crowder*

The 324th Fighter Group gave up its Warhawks for Thunderbolts. By then its P-40Ls, such as this 316th Squadron aircraft at Foggia Main were well worn. The fighter has a fair amount of fresh olive drab paint over past markings, indicating it had served several pilots and squadrons. The Merlin-powered P-40L was a lightweight, extended fuselage (starting with the L-5) version of the F with only four guns, so it was something of a hot rod even at combat weights. *Fred E. Bamberger, Jr.*

Ben Duke and his crew chief sit alert at the 8th
Pursuit Squadron, 49th Pursuit Group revetment at
Strauss Airstrip, 27 miles outside Darwin, Australia,
in early May 1942. The P-40E is covered with

camouflage netting, a very real necessity since
northern Australia was under constant Japanese
attack. *Clyde H. Barnett, Jr.*

Previous page
Clyde Barnett's 8th Squadron, 49th Fighter Group
P-40E sits opposite the alert hut under camouflage
netting at Strauss Airstrip outside Darwin, Australia,
May 1942. Barnett recorded in his diary one day, "I am
sitting in the alert hut at the south end of the strip, on
the 5-minute alert, with Blue Flight. Red Flight is on
15-minute today so get to stay at the mess until
needed." *Clyde H. Barnett, Jr.*

Since he was a West Palm Beach native, Clyde Barnett
painted the appropriate nose art on his 8th Squadron,
49th Fighter Group P-40E. This photo was taken at
Kila Kila, New Guinea, in late 1942. Barnett got four
kills in P-40s—two Betty bombers in April 1942, then
two more Japanese aircraft in 1943—before going
home. *Clyde H. Barnett, Jr.*

Continuing to paint his Warhawk, Clyde Barnett included a scene from West Palm Beach and Donald Duck jabbering from behind the star. The 49th Fighter Group had some particularly colorful P-40s with art appearing at several locations on the aircraft. *Clyde H. Barnett, Jr.*

Next page
Blue Flight, 8th Squadron, 49th Pursuit Group on patrol over Darwin in late- April 1942 when these P-40Es saw quite a bit of action. When Clyde Barnett got his first kill on April 25 he had only twenty-five hours flying time in the P-40. Though a Zero put three holes in his Warhawk, Barnett got a Betty, and his squadron mates managed to come through the combat with excellent results: eight Bettys and three Zeros claimed destroyed. *Clyde H. Barnett, Jr.*

Bruce Harris at the 8th Fighter Squadron alert shack, Kila Kila, New Guinea, late 1942. In many ways the grass huts were an improvement over Army-issue tents but they didn't do much to keep the bugs, snakes, and other wild things out, particularly at night. Unfortunately, there wasn't much to do but live with them since there was no way to kill off an entire jungle of animals. The huts were not bad at beating the daytime heat. *Clyde H. Barnett, Jr.*

The only fighters to get airborne and do any damage during the attack on Pearl Harbor flew out of Haleiwa Strip on the north coast of Oahu. From that point on it became a dispersal point for air defense of the Hawaiian Islands. This P-40K sits in a revetment adjacent to the runway in September 1943, long after the war had gone on to other places. *Via Jack Cook*

A P-40K is pushed back into its revetment at Haleiwa Strip, Oahu, September 1943. Situated among the many trees growing next to the runway, the revetments were quite effective in camouflaging the Warhawks below. After the Pearl Harbor attack, the strip remained a gunnery training facility. *Jack Cook*

Though the P-40 served in all theaters of war except Europe, it will always be associated with China because of the Flying Tigers. Here mechanics work on a 26th Squadron, 51st Fighter Group P-40E in China. This was just about the sum total of facilities and equipment, other than an engine hoist. Discarded 55-gallon drums served as everything from jack stands to lunch tables since so many of them were brought in over the Hump. *USAF via Stan Piet*

Pet monkeys weren't much help in China, but they were a welcome relief from living and fighting on the end of a long and hard-pressed supply line. Sgt. Elmer J. Pence paints a second kill flag on this 26th Squadron, 51st Fighter Group P-40K at Kunming, late 1943, while the monkey stays busy with the artist's paint brush. The Warhawk's paint is much the worse for wear, and the black on the prop tips has been completely scoured off. *USAF*

Pilots and ground crew of the 26th Fighter Squadron seem to enjoy the pet monkey's antics as Sgt. Elmer Pence continues to paint the second kill flag on this P-40K at Kunming, China, in late 1943. The K was the heaviest of all P-40 variants at 10,000 pounds. This didn't do much for performance, in spite of an uprated Allison engine. The best performing Warhawks were the lightweight L, M, and N models, but the P-40 didn't come up to the day's standards until the XP-40Q, which was too late to see World War II service. *USAF via Stan Piet*

A Royal New Zealand Air Force Kittyhawk just airborne off Fighter Strip #1 at Bougainville, Soloman Islands, April 1944. Across the runway from this view out of Garnett Tower are Avengers, Airacobras, and Lightnings. The largest island in the Solomon chain, Bougainville was invaded by the Allies on 1 November 1943 to provide a staging base for the bombing of Rabaul. Though the last major Japanese counterattack was made in late January 1945, there were skirmishes until the end of the war. *National Archives*

A Merlin-powered P-40F on a test flight out of Buffalo in 1942. Though the first batch of aircraft had the short fuselage of the E model, a little over half the F production run incorporated a 20-inch extension as an attempt to eliminate tail flutter. The modification gave the fighter better stability, particularly on the ground during take-off and landing. Since the engine was based on the low-altitude Merlin 28 there was basically no performance improvement compared to the F's Allison-powered brothers. *NASM Arnold Collection*

A 3rd Air Commando Group P-40N flies over Alligator Point, Florida, in August 1944 as the unit trains for combat. Before heading for the Philippines, the Group would transition to the P-51 Mustang under the command of Maj. Walker "Bud" Mahurin, a famous Thunderbolt ace with the 56th Fighter Group in the European Theatre. *Jacques Young*

A P-40F undergoes field maintenance with about as many tools as could be expected under combat conditions. A liquid-cooled fighter was certainly more complex to work on than an air-cooled type. The plumbing alone for what was often referred to as the "hot water toilet," was a twisting, turning series of pipes and rubber hoses that always seemed to be in the hardest places to reach, much less get a wrench on. *USAF*

Previous page
This flight of advanced transition fighters out of
Randolph Field, Texas, consists of a P-40K, a P-40R-1,
and a P-40R-2. A total of 300 long fuselage P-40Fs and
Ls, originally slated for Merlin engines, were modified
to take Allison V-1710-81s of 1,360 horsepower and
were then redesignated R-1 and R-2 respectively for
use in stateside training. A quick way to spot what used
to be an F or an L is to look at the wing guns. The F
carried three .50s in each wing, while the L carried only
two in each wing. These two Rs reflect the difference
upon close examination. *USAF*

A P-40E Warhawk gets up and away on a training
flight in the U.S. The pilot is wearing his overseas cap
and a pair of headphones—ear and head protection was
still something yet to be designed into regulation issue
equipment. The flight leader's stripe would soon
disappear, resurrected (unofficially) only in the last
year of the war in the Pacific, particularly on P-38s.
NASM Arnold Collection via Stan Piet

A brand new P-40N over upper New York state during a test flight out of the Curtiss factory at Buffalo. This final production version of the Warhawk was another attempt at getting as much performance as possible from the basic design. Again, saving weight was the primary thrust of the effort. Only four guns with reduced ammunition capacity were carried on these, along with aluminum oil coolers and radiators, lighter wheels, smaller fuel tank, and the same 1,200-horsepower engine fitted to the M. The result was a boost in speed to 378 miles per hour, the fastest of all models, but still far below the competition. With the P-40N-5 came a return to six guns and the improved-vision canopy that made the N so recognizable. In the end more Ns were built—5,215—than any other P-40. The last of the line, P-40N-40-CU AAF 44-47964, rolled out of Buffalo on 30 November 1944. *NASM Arnold Collection*

Gunnery training at Punta Gorda, Florida, in 1944, was centered around the P-40Ns sent brand new from the factory. With the massive output of Warhawks going on unabated, most were sent to the advanced fighter training fields in the U.S., a boon to pilots since, up to mid-1943, most of the aircraft fighter pilots learned on were worn out from hard use. Some were even war wearies returned from the active theaters. Flying a new P-40 was intoxicating; not only was the Allison and its systems virtually trouble-free, but the light controls and maneuverability of the Curtiss were an invitation to push one's limits. *John Quincy via Stan Wyglendowski*

When Army pilot Class 43-K showed up at Napier Field, Alabama, in November 1943 to go through gunnery training and fighter transition, they found these parrot-headed P-40Ns on the line. For all the shark mouths on P-40s, few could equal the color and originality of these "birds." *James G. Weir*

One of the 43-K pilots with his parrot-headed P-40N at Napier Field, Alabama, November or December 1943. The line chiefs must have had some dedicated nose artists to paint these involved and eye-catching parrots. *James G. Weir*

Jim Weir, Army pilot Class 43-K, climbs up on his parrot-headed P-40N at Napier Field, Alabama, November or December 1943. The feathers extend back to the windshield, giving the bird a real sense of flying through the air. It must have been great fun to fly one of these colorful Warhawks straight out of Advanced. *James G. Weir*

The only other pressing contract at Curtiss' Buffalo plant, in addition to the P-40, was the C-46 Commando transport, developed out of a civil airliner prototype. The aircraft was massive, clearly evident here flying with a new P-40F in early 1942. With two R-2800 engines, it was essentially a four-engine type with two oversized powerplants. This gave the C-46 a tremendous carrying capacity, more than proved later in the war when it became the single most important aircraft flying the Hump from India to China. *NASM Arnold Collection via Stan Piet*

What a surprise! When the first American fighter pilots started to wander around the airfields near Tokyo they came across an old friend. This P-40E among the ruins was one of several captured by the Japanese when they overran the Philippines and Java. Much as the Allies did during the war, enemy aircraft were restored and test flown to compare performance against line types that would be facing them. Since spares became a real issue, these fighters were often retired after short evaluation periods and then pushed aside to rot. *James G. Weir*

The unusual yellow paint job on this stateside P-40N is marred only by the camouflaged replacement cowling. Quite often the commanders of fighter transition units could paint their airplanes any way they wanted, resulting in some very interesting hot rods. *W. J. Balogh via David W. Menard*

Next page
When Fred Dyson purchased what was left of the RCAF Kittyhawk inventory on 23 October 1947, he, in a single stroke, saved much of the present P-40 population. He barged the fighters across the river from Canada to Washington state, moved them to Boeing Field, Seattle, then La Guardia, then sold them off one at a time. By 1950, one of these Kittys, AL152, was spraying crops for Washington County, Colorado, as N1207V. On 31 January 1958 it was bought by Frank Tallman and based at Palwaukee Airport, Illinois, until Tallman moved to California, where the aircraft is seen here in January 1961. *Dustin W. Carter via Dick Phillips*

Previous page
When Frank Tallman and Paul Mantz formed their
movie-making and museum venture, Tallmantz
Aviation/Movieland of the Air, at Orange County
Airport, California, one of the finest collections of
vintage aircraft was created. Here N1207V sits in front
of the main office, much the worse for wear, in March
1964. By this time the original canopy had been lost in
flight and a bogus N model replacement was attached,
though it did not fit well at all. For the most part,
Tallman flew the P-40E with no canopy at all.
Jeff Ethell

Surplus P-40s became just about everything, including
gas station decorations like this 40E at Everett,
Washington, 7 August 1965. This was just about the
time ex-military junk was being labeled "warbirds."
a term which stuck as the generic label for the
movement. When someone managed to talk the owner
out of his billboard, the fighter was gone through and
put back in the air with Dave Tallichet's Yesterday's
Air Force. It then ended up in the hands of Brian
O'Farrell who sold it to Dick Hansen who now flies it
as a representation of Col. Bob Scott's *Old
Exterminator. Fred Johnsen*

Here's N1207V a few years later at Orange County Airport in June 1966 (when Tallmantz was in decline) with a different paint job (an RAF scheme for a few scenes in the movie *Tobruk*). The N canopy has been modified to fit the E fuselage. The Warhawk had already been mortgaged off to Rosen-Novak Auto Co., Omaha, the previous February, and on 29 May 1968 it was auctioned to A. R. Woodson for $7,000. After a long rebuild it flew in 1973 and was sold to Eric Mingledorff in 1984, then John MacGuire in July 1986. The two-seat TP-40N in the background was bought from Movieland of the Air by Kermit Weeks who will have it on airworthy display at his museum near Disney World. *Jeff Ethell*

This Fred Dyson Kitty went to several owners until being rebuilt as a corporate two-seater by Continental Steel Buildings, Burbank, California, in 1950 and 1951. Gil Macy, Montery, California, bought the aircraft in 1963 after it was damaged in an accident and flew it on the West Coast as a show plane. He leased it to 20th Century Fox as one of the airworthy P-40Es for the movie *Tora, Tora, Tora,* and the film folks managed to damage it. Tom Camp bought it in 1972 and rebuilt it (here it is with his initials on the side in November 1974) before selling it to Don Anklin in 1978, who then sold it to Flying Tiger Airlines. *Dustin W. Carter*

A boy's dream sits derelict at Pompano Beach, Florida, December 1965. Another of Fred Dyson's barged Kittyhawks, AK827 became a cloud seeder with Weather Mod Co. in Redlands, California. It was sold to Bill Ruch at Pompano in 1959 and slowly rotted away until the late Bill Ross bought the fighter in 1969. It wasn't until it was sold to Charles Nichols in 1977 that a full restoration (helped by P-40 aficionado John Paul) was started at his Yankee Air Corps, Chino, California. *David Ostrowski*

Late-March 1976: Bob Conrad straps into Ed Maloney's Planes of Fame P-40N at Indian Dunes Airstrip, California, before shooting a scene for the TV movie "Baa Baa Black Sheep," the pilot for the Black Sheep Squadron TV series very loosely based on the life of Marine Corps ace Greg "Pappy" Boyington, played by Robert Conrad. The Warhawk (AAF 42-105192, RCAF 858) is yet another of Fred Dyson's recovered fighters that ended up as a cloud seeder with Weather Modification Co. in 1956. After it crashed in 1958, Ed Maloney obtained the remains, and another derelict was made airworthy, as it remains today at Chino. *Harold R. Knowles*

When the RCAF sold their Kittyhawks in 1946, most went to Fred Dyson in Seattle. However, a few intrepid Canadians forked out their money, among them George Maude who bought P-40E AK803 (RCAF 1034) from war assets at Pat Bay Field for $50 in August 1946. He was so happy with the fighter, which had just over 500 hours total time, that he put in a bid for another at $65, just to be sure he got it. Much to his chagrin, he was outbid by $10! The Kitty, which had been stripped of its camouflage paint and polished for a 1945 war bond tour, came with ammo feed chutes and boxes, a working reflector gun sight, a zero-time Allison, and numerous spares, everything except the guns. Since that time Maude has been the sole owner of 1034, kept in a hangar near his Sidney, British Columbia, home. He runs 1034 up several times a year, operates all the systems, and keeps it in fighting trim. The aircraft's war history includes service in Alaska in the spring of 1942 with No.118 Squadron, then air defense patrols with Nos.132 and 133 Squadrons through 1945. Maude's untouched Kittyhawk is a glimpse at time standing still. *George Maude*

P-51 MUSTANG

Jeffrey L. Ethell

Chapter 1

World War II and the Postwar Years

Foaling of a Mustang

"Sired by the English out of an American mother," said Assistant US Air Attache in London, Maj. Thomas Hitchcock, in 1942. The North American P-51 Mustang, against steep odds, emerged at the end of World War II as the finest all-around piston-engine fighter in service.

During the first months of the war the British and French renewed their efforts to purchase US-built aircraft, settling on the P-40. Lt. Benjamin S. Kelsey, head of the Army Air Corps Pursuit Projects Office at Wright Field, and his boss, Col. Oliver P. Echols regretted this since it would push a new Curtiss fighter, the XP-46, off the assembly lines. Air Corps commander Gen. H. H. "Hap" Arnold decided he could not spare the four-month lag in production to change from the P-40 to the P-46—if America were drawn into the war, quantity would be drastically needed.

In January 1940, recalled Kelsey, "Echols made a suggestion to the Anglo-French Purchasing Commission to find a manufacturer who wasn't already bogged down in high-priority stuff. Curtiss-Wright and the Air Corps would make available all the data we had on the XP-46 to help them build a new fighter. This was our secret talk in the halls to get P-46s in place of the P-40, to find some way of getting around the problem."

Opposite page
P-51Cs of the 51st Fighter Group on the line at Kunming, China, 1945. Originally assigned to the Tenth Air Force with P-40s, the group was transferred to the Fourteenth Air Force in October 1943 to defend the eastern end of the route over the Hump. By the time the 51st was given Mustangs in 1945 the group was harassing Japanese shipping in the Red River delta and supporting Chinese ground troops in their drive along the Salween River. *US Air Force*

First filly in a long long line of thorough-breds—the NA-73X during an early test flight, most likely in the spring of 1941 after it was rebuilt following a crash landing on 20 November 1940. Though the Army Air Corps was not the direct buyer, the regulation red, white, and blue stripes have been painted on the rudder. *North American via Larry Davis*

Scouting for other companies to build the P-40, the commission was drawn to North American Aviation, which had done a sterling job in providing Harvard trainers. The company made it clear they had no desire to build another firm's fighter; they wanted to design one themselves.

Commission member Sir Henry Self approached North American president James H. "Dutch" Kindelberger about designing such a fighter. By April 1940 NAA Vice President J. Leland Atwood had negotiated an agreement. Donovan R. Berlin, designer of the P-40, had spent the better part of the past two years developing the XP-46. With his go-ahead, Atwood bought the data, along with the results of how the aborted belly radiator scoop worked on the original XP-40, for $56,000. On 4 May, North American signed a Foreign Release Agreement with the Air Corps permitting sale of the Model NA-73 overseas, providing that two examples were supplied to the Army. Kelsey and Echols had maneuvered hard to get their new fighter built at a time when the Air Corps had no procurement money.

North American's Chief Engineer Raymond Rice and his team, under Chief Designer Edgar Schmued, began a seven-day work week to produce the fighter. Wing designer Larry Waite incorporated, at the insistence of Edward Horkey (aerodynamicist), the NACA (National Advisory Committee for Aeronautics) laminar-flow wing section, which had not been in the original design concept. Kelsey had pushed behind the scenes with NACA's Eastman Jacobs to get the new wing design into the project, and soon Jacobs was with the North American team on the West Coast. "All this happened," recalled Kelsey, "without anybody at Wright Field

having the foggiest notion of what was going on. We had to stay out of it because it was a British procurement." The North American team's genius resulted in the best design possible around the radical NACA laminar-flow wing section.

Though the Curtiss data was shipped by crate to California, Atwood later said not much of it was used in the final design. Others inside the industry, particularly Don Berlin and others at Curtiss, said otherwise from the time the Mustang became famous.

The first production Mustang, AG345, high in the southern California skies. After the crash of the NA-73X, the lagging flight-test schedule was commenced with AG345, which was flown for the first time by Louis Wait on 23 April 1941. It was subsequently retained by North American Aviation (NAA) for project testing. *John Quincy via Stan Wyglendowski*

There was no 120-day requirement for completion of the prototype, as has often been asserted. The only completion date

A Mustang IA in RAF service. The basic difference between the Mustang I, which went operational in mid-1942, and the IA was armament. The Mustang I had four .50 caliber and four .30 caliber machine guns, while the IA had four 20mm cannon. The RAF and RCAF pilots flying these early Army Co-Operation Command Mustangs at low level knew they had a real winner, particularly in speed. Very few fighters could keep up with the early Allison powered Mustangs on the deck. *Robert Astrella*

noted in the contract was initial delivery by January 1941 and all 400 aircraft delivered by September 30, 1941. Using internal systems and components from the Harvard trainer such as hydraulics, wheels, brakes, and electrics, the men at North American pushed the NA-73X out of the shop in a remarkable 102 days, minus the engine, which arrived twenty days later. It was not until 26 October 1940 that Vance Breese took the prototype into the air from Mines Field, California, for the first time.

The ventral radiator scoop for oil and glycol cooling needed aerodynamic refinement. The problems it caused weren't

When the 631st Fighter-Bomber Squadron (Dive) was working up in the United States, its pilots flew a number of different fighters to gain experience. This A-36A Invader is carrying blue practice bombs at one of the small dirt strips the unit used in 1943. By the time the outfit was flying P-39s, it had been merged with the 630th Squadron to form the 514th Squadron of the 406th Fighter Group, which would convert to P-47s before going overseas. *John Quincy via Stan Wyglendowski*

Women Airforce Service Pilots (WASPs) Barbara Jane Erickson (left) and Evelyn Sharp (right) discuss flying the P-51A Mustang with Lt. Grover Bryon at Long Beach, California, June 1942. The WASPs did a tremendous job ferrying all types of Army aircraft, from PT-19s to B-29s, though they were never officially inducted into the service. Evelyn was later killed ferrying a P-38 Lightning. Barbara was awarded the Air Medal in 1943 for making four transcontinental flights in a little less than five days, ferrying a P-47, P-51, C-47 and P-38. *NASM*

solved until the scoop was redesigned and lowered away from the boundary-layer aerodynamic disturbances on the underside of the fuselage. The initial Mustangs, as a result, did not fully realize the benefit of the "Meredith effect" that resulted in the air exiting the scoop creating thrust, offsetting the drag caused by the scoop.

The first Mustang I, British production number AG345, was first flown on 23 April 1941. The Air Corps was to have received their first example, designated

This A-36A Invader dive-bomber was flown by
John P. "Jeep" Crowder out of Gela, Sicily,
with the 524th Squadron, 27th Fighter-
Bomber Group. Conditions were marginal, to
be kind, and often impossible, alternating
between blowing dust and a sea of mud.
Crowder had entered action with the 33rd
Fighter Group by flying his P-40F off the
carrier *Chenango* to French Morocco in late
1942 before transferring to the 27th to fly the
dive-bomber version of the Mustang. *John P.
Crowder via Dorothy Helen Crowder*

Following pages
Stateside maintenance on a P-51B, 1944.
This working airplane has quite a few stains,
including overflow from the fuel tank filler
neck. The Mustang was a simple aircraft
overall, as can be seen by the yellow and black
flap down indicator markings—there was no
flap indicator in the cockpit, other than the
different detents, or notches, in the flap
handle. *NASM*

One of the first production P-51B-1s, long after its combat career had ended, serving time as a headquarters hack or operational training unit (OTU) machine in late 1944. By this time new P-51Ds were being supplied to fighter groups, though late production P-51Bs and Cs were still operational. The retrofitted Malcolm hood provided much improved pilot visibility and some pilots preferred these aircraft over the later bubble canopy D models. *Robert Astrella*

XP-51, in February 1941 and the other in March, but the first airframe didn't arrive at Wright Field until August 24. The second came in December. Contrary to the long-standing story of official neglect delaying acceptance of the fighter by the newly redesignated Army Air Forces, delays were caused by numerous additional problems, not the least of which was chaos resulting from the bombing of Pearl Harbor eight days before the second XP-51 was delivered. According to a 1942 P-51 acceptance report, production delays, bad weather, gun charging system problems, needed refinements to the Allison engines, and the higher priorities given to other aircraft already being evaluated hampered the process.

On 7 July 1941, over a month before
the first XP-51 arrived at Wright Field,
the AAF placed an order for 150 P-51s to
be furnished to the RAF. Only 93 ended
up with the British. Fifty-five were kept
by the AAF, two being set aside for the
XP-78 project (later XP-51B) to fit a
Packard-built Rolls-Royce Merlin engine
to the airframe. This promising start was

55th Fighter Group buzz job, Wormingford,
England, 1945. This was by far the favorite
sport of fighter pilots in World War II,
regardless of the potential court martial after
it was over. There was something over-
powering about being young and in control
of a multi-thousand horsepower machine.
Robert T. Sand

As with these mechanics working on a 4th
Fighter Group P-51D at Debden, England,
mid 1944, most maintenance was done outside
during World War II, regardless of theater of
operations. Fortunately this is a mild English
summer. *US Air Force*

Another war-weary Mustang, this P-51B-5 was kept on strength with the 20th Fighter Group at Kings Cliffe in late 1944, early 1945, as a run-about and basic joy-rider. There was only so much life in these Mustangs and maintenance priority was always given to combat-capable aircraft. *Robert Astrella*

slowed by lack of funds, since no more money was available in that year's budget for fighter aircraft, but Echols, Kelsey, and Kindelberger found enough money in the attack portion of the AAF budget. The solution was, according to Kelsey, finding

the next number allocated for an aircraft, which happened to be A-36. Adding bomb racks and dive brakes to the airframe—and calling it an attack bomber instead of a fighter—kept the production line open. This risky move by a few maneuvering Army officers showed anything but neglect.

World War II

Before the first P-51 flew, an order was placed for 500 A-36 aircraft on April 16, 1942. By March 1943, when the first AAF Mustangs were ordered into combat in

The 336th Fighter Squadron's hack Mustang was a horse of a different color. The 4th Fighter Group had always been known for doing things with some dash but this two-seater had to be one of the more striking war-weary Mustangs in England, thanks to some dedicated mechanics. The aircraft, coded VF-4, is lined up at Debden with a 359th Fighter Group P-51D and several other Mustangs on 23 March 1945 during a meeting of fighter unit commanders to plan cover for the Rhine River crossing. *Edward B. Richie*

North Africa, the RAF's Army Co-Operation Command had been flying the fighter in combat for 10 months. Though British

Opposite page
Crew chief Johnny Ferra straps 4th Fighter Group ace Don Gentile into *Shangri-La*, the P-51B that Gentile rode to fame for two months from February to April 1944. During a low-level buzz job after the 13 April 1944 mission to Schweinfurt, Gentile misjudged and flew into the ground, destroying his legendary "kite." Group commander Don Blakeslee had said that anyone pranging a kite while stunting would be immediately kicked out of the group. Blakeslee lived up to his word and without even seeing Gentile, booted him out and off to the States. *via Stan Piet*

When Poland was overrun in 1939, many Polish pilots were integrated into the RAF, eventually forming squadrons and flying most of the major British types. By mid-1944 these squadrons were an active part of the RAF's striking power. Some Polish units converted to Mustang IIIs, then IVs, and flew them in combat through the rest of the war on long-range escort and deep fighter penetration. As with most RAF Mustang IIIs, this No. 309 Squadron (Polish) aircraft has been retrofitted with a Malcolm hood. Note the Polish insignia on the lower front engine cowling. *John Quincy via Stan Wyglendowski*

and American pilots found the Mustang to be faster than anything around at low level, it suffered greatly from lack of high altitude performance.

Waiting in the wings was a wizard for the Yank aircraft: just as Merlin was able to transform a young boy into King Arthur, so could the Rolls-Royce wizard of the same name transform a spirited American pony into a fiery thoroughbred.

After flying a Mustang I in April 1942, Rolls-Royce test pilot Ronald W. Harker went back to his company and asked if a Merlin 61 engine could be fitted to the excellent, low-drag Mustang airframe. Harker believed that the combination could result in the best fighter of the war, in spite of the British Air Ministry asking, "Why waste time on an untried, American-built aeroplane?" In spite of much opposition, five aircraft were set aside for modification.

Rolls-Royce let North American know what they were up to, so North American set aside two P-51 airframes to receive the American-built Packard Merlin. A friendly competition developed to see who would be the first to fly a Merlin Mustang. The

A 1st Air Commando Group P-51A flies close escort on former Flying Tiger R. T. Smith's B-25H over Burma. Under the talented leadership of Phil Cochran and Johnny Alison, the 1st became a guerrilla striking force that could hit targets with all manner of aircraft, from L-5s on up, in support of British Brigadier Orde Wingate's Chindits and the US Army's rough jungle war. *R.T. Smith*

A line of new P-51Cs in August 1944 at Dale Mabrey Field, Tallahassee, Florida, await their 3rd Air Commando Group pilots. The unit had just transitioned from P-40s before heading to the Philippines under the command of former Flying Tiger Arvid E. Olson, Jr. *Jacques Young*

British only just beat the Americans— Rolls-Royce flew their first conversion on 14 October 1942, and North American had the XP-51B up on November 30. The results were stunning, and almost exactly one year later the P-51B entered combat over Europe.

In spite of serious teething problems brought on by rushed development, the

The English winter of 1944–1945 was not kind, with the ground covered most of the time by frost or snow. *Rusty* was the P-51K assigned to Jeff French in the 339th Fighter Group at Fowlmere, England. When French finished his tour in January 1945, *Rusty* was reassigned to Bill Preddy, brother of leading Mustang ace George Preddy. Tragically both brothers were killed in action—George by American gunners who mistook his P-51 for a German fighter on Christmas Day 1944, and Bill by enemy fire on 17 April 1945 near Prague. The only difference between the K and D model Mustangs was the propeller: the K had one from the Aeroproducts factory, while the D had a Hamilton Standard with cuffs at the base of each blade.
L. Jeffrey French

213

When John C. Casey was assigned this P-51K at Leiston, he named it after his hometown. The red and yellow striped spinner and checkerboard cowl band were hallmarks of the 357th Fighter Group, one of the most aggressive Eighth Air Force fighter outfits.
Arnold N. Delmonico

Merlin Mustang could fly farther into enemy territory than any other fighter on the same amount of fuel, thus saving the AAF's strategic bombing campaign from annihilation at the hands of the Luftwaffe. By the end of World War II the P-51 reigned supreme on all fronts, its pilots having claimed more than 5,000 enemy aircraft destroyed, more than either the P-38 or the P-47.

The ground crew runs up "Lefty" Grove's 4th Fighter Group P-51D, VF-T, at Debden, England, in early 1945, just before a mission.

The external tanks are hung and serviced and by the time Grove gets there the engine will be warm and ready for restart. *Francis M. Grove*

"Lefty" Grove's 336th Squadron P-51D sits on the line at Debden, England, in early 1945. Spawned from the RAF Eagle Squadrons, the 4th Fighter Group had a distinctive flavor in both its flying and its operational jargon: an airplane was a "kite," the intelligence scoop was the "gen," one didn't crash an airplane, he "pranged his kite." Grove was in front of a long line of replacement pilots who came directly from the United States Army Air Forces rather than through the RAF. *Francis M. Grove*

Mr. Ted belonged to 78th Fighter Group commander Frederic Gray, who was at the helm for almost two years, from May 1943 to February 1945. In that time the Duxford checker-nose gang traded in their P-47s for Mustangs and became one of the Eighth Air Force's premier fighter outfits. *Robert Astrella*

Following pages
An imposing view of a 357th Fighter Group Mustang. Since the clamshell fairing doors have not dropped down yet, the hydraulic system is still under pressure, indicating the aircraft has been run recently, and that the pilot or crew chief has not pulled the hydraulic pressure dump handle in the cockpit.
via Harry Friedman

A 4th Fighter Group P-51—*Nad* has been painted on the side in the distinctive style of Don Allen, the premier nose artist in the group, who was responsible for decorating some of the more famous aircraft in the ETO. *via Harry Friedman*

The Seventh Air Force's P-51Ds had a single job, to escort B-29s on Very Long Range (VLR) missions into Japan and back, often up to ten hours at a time. Though the Mustang had a fine cockpit, it was a very uncomfortable place after a few hours.

This look across the 364th Fighter Group base at Honington, England, in late 1944 shows the life of the enlisted ground crew. On the right are unopened external fuel tank crates. In the background behind the two Mustangs are the gun butts for bore sighting the guns. And to the left is a line shack that was constructed from discarded fuel tank crates. Necessity drove men to find whatever comfort they could on these open fields, particularly in the winter, and the shacks became lifesavers. The bicycles were the standard mode of local transportation, unless one had enough rank to get a jeep. *Mark Brown/US Air Force Academy*

221

Marvin Arthur's *Blondie* was one of the finest of crew chief Don Allen's 4th Fighter Group nose art creations. Though named for Arthur's wife, the nose art came from Allen's imagination, as he recalled "sexy, but covered." *Donald E. Allen*

April 1945, Peretola, Italy. *Tempus Fugut* was the personal P-51D of 31st Fighter Group commander W. A. Daniel. The 31st was famous for flying Spitfires until almost mid-1944, when they transitioned to Mustangs. *Fred Bamberger*

A Chinese American Composite Wing (CACW) P-51D with the gear just about in the wells after takeoff at Nanking, China, in 1945. Within the CACW the 3rd and 5th Fighter Group flew P-40s, then Mustangs through the end of the war, primarily in close bomber-escort and ground attack missions. *George McKay via Larry Davis*

Kiangwan Airfield, Shanghai, 1945. On the line among the B-25s, C-47s, and C-46s are an F-6D Mustang of the 530th Squadron, 311th Fighter Group and a P-47D of the 93rd Squadron, 81st Fighter Group. *George McKay via Larry Davis*

Below
The 23rd Fighter Group was a direct descendant of Claire Chennault's American Volunteer Group, the Flying Tigers, flying P-40s, then P-51s through the end of the war. These 75th Squadron P-51Ds rest on the line in China with Thunderbolts at the end of the war. *George McKay via Larry Davis*

These P-51Ds at Mt. Farm, England, carry the simple 7th Photo Group markings of blue spinner and red cowl stripe, plus the red rudder normally painted on 13th Photo Squadron F-5 Lightnings. In January 1945 the 7th began to receive Mustangs to provide fighter escort for its F-5s, armed with nothing but cameras deep in enemy territory . . . a dangerous job. *Robert Astrella*

Below
The 7th Photo Group recorded 4,251 sorties and fifty-eight aircraft missing in action, among them five P-51s. The Mustangs flew 880 sorties, getting one probable and one damaged while protecting the Lightnings. This 7th P-51D sits at Mt. Farm with full external tanks and "putt-putt" auxiliary power unit on the left ready to plug in for start. The clamshell wheel fairing doors are not fully down, indicating the Mustang was run and warmed up a short time before by its crew chief. *Robert Astrella*

Above
Happy IV was flown by 339th Fighter Group commander William C. Clark. The eleven flags represented one air and ten ground kills while his wife's name, *Dotty*, was painted on the canopy frame. The dispersal area at Fowlmere, like so many other bases around the world, was covered by pierced steel plank (PSP) to prevent the aircraft from getting mired down in the mud. *James R. Starnes/Harry Corry via Robert S. DeGroat*

The 504th Fighter Squadron at dispersal, Fowlmere, summer 1945. The interlocked wooden plank on the ground was an alternative to PSP in keeping fighters free from the clutches of English mud. With the war over, the 339th Fighter Group, along with the rest of the Eighth Air Force, had very little flying to do. Everyone was waiting to go home. *James R. Starnes*

Jerry Collins in his *Lady of the Sky* over Japan in September 1945 with the 3rd Squadron, 3rd Air Commando Group. As the war ended, the Army Air Forces moved into Japan to become a part of the occupation forces with the 3rd going from Ie Shima to Atsugi on 20 September 1945. *Jacques Young*

Left
Triple Threat was a 3rd Squadron, 3rd Air Commando Group P-51D at Chitose, Japan, after the war. The group had many different colored spinners, particularly blue, red, and yellow, but the color on the tail denoted the squadron—blue for the 3rd and red for the 4th. *Paul Vercammen via David W. Menard*

Previous page
R. Vern Blizzard with *Punkie II*, 5Q-O, his 504th Squadron, 339th Fighter Group P-51D, at Fowlmere, England, 1945. Blizzard put his wife's nickname on the Mustang for good luck and apparently it worked since he made it through to the end of the war. *Robert V. Blizzard*

Another 3rd Air Commando Mustang, *Gypsy* had a good representation of Milton Caniff's Miss Lace as nose art. Caniff's creations were extremely popular during World War II, particularly his women, including the Dragon Lady and Burma. *Paul Vercammen via David W. Menard*

Though this shot was posed by the AAF photographer, these 4th Fighter Group armorers at Debden, England give a pretty good idea of the wallop packed by the six .50 caliber machine guns and ammunition that went into a P-51D. *NASM*

By the time World War II was over AAF units were faced with a surplus of aircraft and nowhere to go. These 55th Fighter Group Mustangs sit idle at Wormingford, England, in June 1945 awaiting an inspection. Eventually the '51s were scrapped. *Robert T. Sand*

Left
A late-model P-51D, with a new paddle-blade Hamilton Standard propeller, on the line at Ontario Army Air Base, California, 1945. Ontario was home to a number of AAF training units, flying everything from Stearmans to P-38s to captured enemy aircraft like the Japanese Zero. Most of Southern California was a mass of military training fields during the war, ripe with the opportunity for pilots to bounce each other unannounced. *Norman W. Jackson*

Several Mustangs of the 46th Squadron, 21st Fighter Group sit on the volcanic ash of Iwo Jima in 1945. The Seventh Air Force's P-51Ds had a single job, to escort B-29s on Very Long Range (VLR) missions into Japan and back, often up to ten hours at a time. Though the Mustang had a fine cockpit, it was a very uncomfortable place after a few hours. *Russ Stauffer via John & Donna Campbell*

Below
The cinders and blowing volcanic dust on Iwo Jima took quite a toll on engines and moving parts. The black ash these 72nd Squadron, 21st Fighter Group Mustangs sit on at Iwo was like nothing anyone had ever seen. *Russ Stauffer via John & Donna Campbell*

The flagship, #200, of the 21st Fighter Group, carrying the tail stripe colors of all three squadrons, lands at Tinian in 1945. The group was based at Iwo Jima to provide VLR escort missions for the B-29s of the Twentieth Air Force. *Russ Stauffer via John & Donna Campbell*

New Mustangs at Leyte, October 1945, with nowhere to go and nothing to do. In spite of the war's end, the incredible flow of materiel to the Pacific was hard to shut off, which resulted in new airplanes with no combat time being junked. *D. Watt via David W. Menard*

234

When the 475th Fighter Group let go of its
P-38s after the war, the unit was transitioned
into Mustangs, which quickly got painted up
in their Satan's Angels markings. This 431st
Squadron P-51D in Japan, 1946, reflects the
change. *US Air Force Museum*

Below
In Germany, without a war on, flying time
was cut to the bone and once-fierce Mustangs
were put out to pasture. With the markings
scrubbed off and her paint peeling, it's hard to
tell if this P-51D belonged to the 363rd
Fighter Group or the 354th Fighter Group—
both had yellow nose markings like this. It
really didn't matter. *Tootsie* was broken apart,
burned, and left where she sat in Germany.
Fagen via David W. Menard

Even in the very late 1940s wartime
Mustangs could be seen rotting away, clearly
evident here at the University of Illinois
Airport in 1949. These were stateside training
P-51Cs acquired for the local tech school.
C. Grahan via David W. Menard

Right
Postwar air racing was dominated by
Mustangs, particularly the Thompson and
Bendix races which centered around
Cleveland. The greatest winner of them all
was Hollywood stunt pilot Paul Mantz who
won the Bendix three years in a row with his
P-51Cs, among them the great No. 60 seen
here just after landing. The oil and exhaust
trails tell the story of this cross-country race
from California—push the power as far as the
engine could stand and don't back it off until
landing. *via Walter E. Ohlrich, Jr.*

One of the most radically modified of the racing Mustangs was the stunning, dark green *Beguine*, which was entered in the 1949 Thompson. The belly scoop radiators were removed and installed in the wingtips in hopes of reducing drag. Though there was great anticipation over how the ex-fighter would do, pilot Bill Odom crashed into a house on the course after cutting a pylon, killing himself, a mother and her child. Unlimited air racing was over until 1964 with the advent of less populated courses and a dimming public memory of the crash's innocent victims. *via Walter W. Ohlrich, Jr.*

The name *City of Lynchburg* was carried on all of Woody Edmundson's racing Mustangs, including No. 15 here at Cleveland for the 1947 Thompson Trophy race. With surplus P-51s available all day long for $1,500, there was quite a field for each of the post-war races, painted in all kinds of garish schemes. This sunburst pattern was typical of most airshow aircraft during the period. *Ole C. Griffith*

As bombing distances grew ever longer during World War II, planners called for fighters that could stay with the bombers on extended-range missions. North American offered what was, basically, two lightweight P-51Fs attached, carrying two pilots, with P-51H outer wing panels and engines—the XP-82 Twin Mustang, which flew for the first time on 16 June 1945. This is the first P-82E.
Ron Picciani

Betty Jo, a P-82B, taxies in at New York in 1947 after setting a record by flying 5,000 miles from Hawaii nonstop. In addition to the four underwing external fuel tanks, more tanks were added behind each pilot. It was an epic flight, giving the new US Air Force much-needed publicity for its long-range bomber-escort program during the postwar cutbacks. *NASM*

A line of 27th Fighter-Escort Group P-82Es at Howard AFB, Panama. The "Double-Breasted Mustangs" in the foreground were attached to the 524th Squadron. The first Twin Mustangs were delivered to the 27th in March 1948 to escort the newly created Strategic Air Command's B-29s, B-50s, and B-36s until the summer of 1950 when the redesignated 27th Wing began to receive F-84E Thunderjets. *Ray Williams/Warren Thompson via Don Spry*

The postwar growth of the US Air Force, born out of the wartime US Army Air Forces in 1947, centered around SAC's long-range-bomber capability. This gave urgent life to the F-82E. These 27th Fighter-Escort Group Twin Mustangs have just left Bergstrom Air Force Base, Texas, on a long-range-escort mission carrying extensive external fuel. *B. Mitchell via David W. Menard*

The 52nd All Weather Group at Mitchel Field, Long Island, flew colorful F-82F all-weather interceptors (the new term for night fighters) with radar pods mounted under the center wing. The right cockpit was reconfigured for a radar operator, while the pilot handled the flying from the left. *Ron Picciani*

Post-war decision making on a standard fighter for Reserve and Air National Guard units led to the P-51 being kept while other leftover piston fighters were given to other countries or scrapped. There were brand-new P-51Ds at every turn so it didn't take long to spread them out to many different squadrons across the country. Mustangs would stay in service with the Guard until 1957.
W. J. Balogh via David W. Menard

Air National Guard units came up with imaginative schemes for their F-51Ds but none more so than the Kentucky boys' target sleeve tug, done up in bright yellow, at the ANG gunnery meet at Boise, Idaho, in October 1954. *P. Paulsen via David W. Menard*

The West Virginia Air National Guard was the last ANG unit to fly the F-51D. The Coonskin Boys' colorful postwar period is well reflected by these two Mustangs over the Mountain State. The extended blue nose was inspired by WVANG pilot Edwin L. Heller who originally flew with the 352nd Fighter Group in World War II, the "Blue Nosed Bastards of Bodney." The 167th Fighter Squadron's rampant unicorn jumping past a lightning bolt was the insignia of the old wartime 369th Squadron, 359th Fighter Group, which had been reassigned to the West Virginia unit. Both combat traditions were carried over with much pride. *Ken Hoylman via David W. Menard*

During 1949 inauguration ceremonies for President Harry Truman, WVANG F-51Ds flew escort for B-29s and B-36s as they passed over the ceremony, the last mass piston fly-over of any size for the nation's capital. A short time later the colorful World War II-inspired markings would disappear and an era came to an end. *Ken Hoylman via David W. Menard*

Below
Maj. John B. England taxies out at Nellis Air Force Base, Nevada, 1950, in the lead Mustang of the Red Devils aerobatic team, a forerunner of the jet teams to come. England, who was credited with 17.5 kills with the 357th Fighter Group in World War II, was as colorful as the water-based paint on his F-51, which was painted a solid red. The three wingmen were painted partially red. The paint didn't last long but it could easily be reapplied for the next show. *G. Gravenstine via David W. Menard*

An F-51D of the Minnesota ANG runs up in the winter cold with long-range, jet-style external fuel tanks typical of 1950s-era Mustangs in military service. Though the Guard used both the F-51 and F-47, the Thunderbolt disappeared almost overnight while the Mustang survived to make its way into the civil inventory. Pilots going to Korea would soon regret the Jug's demise. *via Dick Phillips*

Those Mustangs that were kept in the regular Air Force had their share of colorful markings as well. This F-51D at Luke Air Force Base, Arizona, carries the yellow and black checkerboards of the Fighter Weapons School, a tradition carried on to the present day. By the end of the Korean War the last Mustang had been retired from the US Air Force with only the Guard to carry on. *David W. Menard Collection*

The Kentucky ANG lined up at Boise, Idaho, 1954, during annual gunnery training revealed quite a variety in colors and markings, down to the yellow target-sleeve tug at the end. *P. Paulsen via David W. Menard*

As the F-51H was phased out of the active US Air Force inventory into the Guard, pilots were impressed with its hot-rod performance. The only production lightweight Mustang, it served escort-fighter duty with SAC, but there were never enough built to provide spares for an extended service life. The Maryland ANG flew them extensively, at one time putting up a four-ship aerobatic team known as the Guardian Angels. *Ron Picciani*

For several years Grumman Aircraft Corporation flew an F-51H as a chase plane for its new jet fighters. The excellent acceleration and top speed of the last Mustang gave Grumman pilots quite a credible chase capability until lack of spares and overhaul facilities made them put the worn-out warhorse to pasture. *H.G. Martin via David W. Menard*

Chapter 2

The Mustang in the Korean War

When the Korean War broke out, the Mustang was thrown straight back into action as the F-51, along with its bigger brother, the F-82 Twin Mustang. The US Air Force had been born in 1947 and the next year P for Pursuit changed to F for Fighter in the Air Force aircraft-designation system. When North Korean Yak fighters strafed Kimpo Airfield on 27 June 1950, F-82s shot down three of them to make the first kills of the war. Though taking a prop driven fighter into a jet war seemed like going backwards, the Mustangs could loiter over ground targets for an hour while the jets could only stay fifteen minutes if they were lucky. The F-51 and F-82 could also use shorter runways, which were usually closer to the front lines.

Unfortunately, the Mustang's liquid cooling system was very vulnerable to damage from ground fire, and many Mustang pilots were killed or became POWs who would not have gone down had they been flying an air-cooled fighter. Though not assigned to the air-to-air combat role, F-51 pilots did tangle with Yaks, shooting down at least four, and the MiG-15, though none of the jets were shot down. Still this wonderful fighter of a bygone era was an antique in the jet age.

Pilots not used to the torque problems in a high-powered piston fighter tended to wreck them regularly, particularly if they had been accustomed to flying with their

Opposite page
No.2 Squadron, South African Air Force, F-51Ds marshall for takeoff on a strike out of Chinhae during the Korean War. They carry the standard close-air-support armament of 500 pound bombs, two five-inch rockets under each wing and full ammunition. A number of Mustang units flew from Chinhae, making logistical support a bit simpler—though nothing was simple in this so-called "limited war." *US Air Force*

This F-82G, *Bucket of Bolts*, made the first kill of the Korean War while attached to the 68th Fighter (All Weather) Squadron. On 27 June 1950 Lts. William Hudson and Carl Fraser downed a Yak-7U in the morning during an attack on Kimpo Airfield by five enemy aircraft. Before the day was over another two aircraft were shot down by Twin Mustangs. *Boardman C. Reed via Don Spry*

feet on the floor. From January 1950 to January 1952 there were 462 major Mustang accidents, over half due to pilot error. Combat losses were even heavier and the Air Force had to pour a continual stream of replacement aircraft and pilots into the fighter-bomber units. By mid-war, all the Mustangs were withdrawn after fighting the very contest most pilots knew to be the most dangerous in World War II: at

low level, antiaircraft fire always had, and always would, take more lives than enemy fighters.

Another view of *Bucket of Bolts,* the Twin Mustang that made the first kill of the Korean War on 27 June 1950. Here she rests at K-2, Taegu, on 16 June 1951 after a year in combat. Twin Mustangs were used primarily for ground support, though night fighting capability was retained to deal with nuisance raids from Bed Check Charlies which droned over to rob people of sleep. *Boardman C. Reed via Dave McLaren*

A 40th Squadron, 35th Fighter Group F-51D has just pulled to a stop on the ramp in Japan, 1950, as the ground crewman moves to chock the wheels. The 35th's squadrons formed the basis for the initial cadre of pilots to take the Mustang back into combat when the Korean War broke out. *Ray Stewart / Warren Thompson via Tom Foote*

Below
The 40th Fighter Squadron line at Johnson Field, Japan, early 1950. The pre-World War II-style rudder stripes were a part of the 35th Fighter Group's colors before the Korean War broke out but they would soon disappear as Mustangs were pressed back into the close-air-support role, one for which it was ill suited due to the vulnerability of its liquid cooling system. *Paul Wilkins via Tom Foote*

Maj. William O'Donnell, commander of the 36th Fighter-Bomber Squadron, runs up *Mac's Revenge*, named for his niece. The other side of the airplane was labled by the crew chief as *O'l Anchor Ass*. The 8th Fighter Group had been flying F-80C Shooting Stars, but with the beginning of the Korean War the jets were taken away and replaced by the Mustangs the pilots had thought were well behind them. The 36th Squadron insignia leers from beneath the name. *William J. O'Donnell*

As a radio change is made on Bill O'Donnell's 36th Squadron F-51D at Tsuiki, Japanese personnel are busy polishing the skin of the aircraft to a bright mirror finish. The Japanese were known for their skill at making Mustangs shine by using quantities of fuller's earth as a very fine, almost talcum powder consistency, abrasive. The results drew a consistent business for the Japanese who were happy for the extra wages. *William J. O'Donnell*

Napalm-loading operations on the 36th Fighter-Bomber Squadron line at Tsuiki. Japanese girls are rolling fuel barrels across the ramp so the jellied gasoline mixture can be loaded into the drop tanks. For such a simple procedure, the results were frightening on the other end. *William J. O'Donnell*

Robert "Pancho" Pasqualicchio with his 67th Fighter-Bomber Squadron F-51D, *OL' NaD-SoB*, at Chinhae, Korea, in 1951. Other 18th Fighter-Bomber Group Mustangs, painted with sharkmouths, can be spotted in the background. The 18th did a sterling job of ground support under an aggressive commander. Though the Mustang was a hold-over from a previous war, air-to-ground delivery techniques had not changed and the prop driven aircraft actually had better accuracy than the jets. Unfortunately the loss rates were horrendous. "I'd have bought my own P-47 at that point!" recalled Pasqualicchio. *Pancho Pasqualicchio*

Col. William "Willy" P. McBride, 18th Fighter-Bomber Group commander, got shot up during a ground-attack mission and had to make a forced landing at K-16, Yongdungpo, in May 1951. The fire crews did an outstanding job of making sure there would be no fire. *Pancho Pasqualicchio*

Chinhae, spring 1951: the unforgiving results of inexperience in high-performance piston fighters. A No. 2 Squadron, South African Air Force, ex-Sunderland flying boat pilot came to Korea with eight to ten hours in Spitfires, made a single familiarization flight in an F-51, then launched on his first combat mission fully loaded with bombs and rockets. He failed to hold the torque on takeoff, pulled to the left, and went into a group of twenty parked reserve-pool Mustangs. The pilot was killed instantly and several F-51s were lost. *Pancho Pasqualicchio*

Col. Rog Mercer in his 187th Fighter
Squadron, ANG, Mustang over the United
States. Many Air National Guard units flying
the F-51 were recalled to Korea, along with
pilots who had piston experience, to fill out the
Mustang groups going to combat. *Pancho
Pasqualicchio*

Right
Kimpo Airfield, South Korea, 1951: the
name on this 45th Tactical Reconnaissance
Squadron RF-51D, *Tulie, Scotty & ?*, referred
to the pilot's kids and pregnant wife. The 45th
had the very dangerous job of photographing
North Korean positions, convoys, and
movements up close with the rear-fuselage-
mounted cameras. Though bombs and rockets
could be carried, and often were, the
squadron's real value lay in providing close to
real-time intelligence for immediate strikes.
In World War II, the tac recce version of the
Mustang was known as the F-6. *Ron Picciani*

The first South Korean pilots to strike back after the North Korean invasion belonged to the Republic of Korea Air Force (ROKAF) 1st Fighter Squadron , flying F-51Ds with US Air Force leadership. The unit, initially trained under the command of Maj. Dean Hess in 1950, grew into an entire wing of Mustangs. This is the ROKAF line at Kangnung late in the war. *Alan Grindberg*

A ROKAF Mustang taxies in from a mission against North Korean positions. South Korean pilots who had wartime experience flying with the Japanese came up to speed in the F-51D relatively fast, whereas other newly trained pilots were almost overwhelmed with the demands of combat until getting enough time with their American advisors. *Ron Picciani*

An 8th Fighter-Bomber Group F-51D just
after shutdown at K-2, Taegu, 2 July 1951.
The ground crew has chocked the Mustang
and is standing by to help the pilot unstrap.
Flying the Mustang in Korea was rough, dirty
work with very little reward. The jet units,
particularly those flying F-86s over MiG Alley,
got most of the glory while the majority of the
war was an air-to-ground campaign. *Boardman C. Reed via Dave McLaren*

274

Jeannie, a 67th Fighter-Bomber Squadron F-51D, gets some much-needed maintenance at Chinhae. Conditions that World War II crews thought they'd never see again reappeared on the rugged, cold airfields of Korea where maintenance took place outside, and mechanics fought frost bite to work on their "antiques" from another war. *US Air Force*

Below
A 39th Squadron, 18th Fighter-Bomber Group F-51D has just taxied in at Chinhae, summer 1951, after a sortie. All of the underwing stores are gone and the residue from the .50 caliber machine guns has spread back across the wing. Mustangs in Korea were worked hard, taking heavy losses. *US Air Force*

RF-51Ds of the 45th Tactical Reconnaissance Squadron taxi out for a mission. Tac recce aircraft relied more on cameras than bombs and rockets. The idea was to loiter in enemy territory, photographing enemy positions and movements, strafing if necessary. The roaming fighters brought back a continual flow of pinpointed targets for concentrated strikes. *US Air Force*

Laborers load a No. 77 Squadron, Royal Australian Air Force F-51D with napalm at the 35th Fighter Group's Korean base. The jellied gasoline was pumped into large drop tanks already hung on the bomb racks; then an ignitor fuse was screwed in just before takeoff. *Gerald Brown*

Chapter 3

Postwar Foreign Service

By the end of the Korean War the Mustang had seen its last days fighting for the United States. Quite a number of F-51s were given to the Reserves and Air National Guard, where they served until 1957, but the majority went overseas under the Military Assistance Plan. An impressive list of foreign air forces were equipped with Mustangs, beginning with those allies that got the fighter in World War II: England, France, Australia, China, South Africa, Russia, South Korea, Taiwan, Philippines, Indonesia, Sweden, Switzerland, Italy, New Zealand, Israel, Canada, Haiti, Uruguay, Guatemala, Nicaragua, Costa Rica, Bolivia, Cuba, Venezuela, and the Dominican Republic.

Not until 1983 were the last active military Mustangs retired from service when the Dominican Republic traded them in for jets. The Mustang had been on continuous active duty forty-three years. From neglected foal to temperamental thoroughbred to charging warhorse, North American Aviation's P-51 Mustang became one of the greatest fighters of all time.

Opposite page
The Dominican Republic was one of the major foreign users of the Mustang, buying most of Sweden's postwar inventory (forty-two aircraft), then from several other air forces, and finally rebuilt from the Cavalier Aircraft Corporation under the Military Assistance Program. This photo shows the alert line at Santiago, Dominican Republic, the forward operating base closest to Cuba, May 1982. At this point in their career the Fuerza Aerea Dominicana (FAD) had used the Mustang as their primary fighter for thirty years, the longest continuous military use of the fighter on record. *Author*

As the Mustang was phased out of first-line US Air Force service, many foreign air forces continued to fly them. These Royal Canadian Air Force Mustangs have just been sold surplus after a long and happy career with pilots who were fiercely proud of their mounts. *Ron Picciani*

January 1963: this P-51D is still in first-line service with Guatemala, but the shiny T-33s in the background are a good indication of what is taking place. Soon all the Mustangs would be gone and the jet age would fully arrive in this small Central American country. *Robb Satterfield*

The Philippine Air Force used the F-51 as a primary fighter into the mid-1950s with the 6th, 7th and 8th Squadrons, 5th Fighter Wing. The wing commander's Mustang sits on the line at Nichols Field, 20 July 1958, with an 8th Squadron aircraft next to it. By 1959 the last P-51s were gone, replaced by F-86 Sabres. *Merle Olmsted*

Index